Shlomo A. Sharlin
Florence W. Kaslow
Helga Hammerschmidt

Together Through Thick and Thin
A Multinational Picture of Long-Term Marriages

"**A**t last, an extensive multinational study of what's right about marriages, rather than what's wrong! Over the years there have been a handful of studies . . . that have attempted to identify the components of an enduring and satisfying marriage. *Together Through Thick and Thin* by Sharlin, Kaslow, and Hammerschmidt reports the results of a study of 610 long-term marriages in eight different countries. The research is well-grounded in theory and employs both established measures and checklists created for this study. The results point to a universal set of ingredients in long-lasting relationships across cultures. In a time when constructionists suggest there is no objective truth regarding a good marriage, it is comforting to find a large cross-cultural sample that endorses a common set of values as necessary for a satisfying relationship. This book can serve as an invaluable guide to the marital therapist in establishing treatment goals universal to happy marriages."

Carol L. Philpot, PsyD
Dean and Professor,
Florida Institute of Technology,
School of Psychology

"**T**his is a landmark study with far-reaching clinical and scientific implications. Three noted family researchers (Israeli, American, and German) used standard inventories with 610 couples from eight countries, with participants' marriages lasting from 20 to 46 years.

Each chapter is lively and enlightening, with Chapter 7, 'Cross-Cultural Analysis,' providing a unique overview from all eight countries. This compact volume is indispensable for students, therapists, and researchers across the entire spectrum of family studies."

Terence Patterson, EdD, ABPP
President-elect,
APA Division of Family Psychology;
Director of Training,
Counseling Psychology
Doctoral Program,
University of San Francisco

Together Through Thick and Thin
A Multinational Picture of Long-Term Marriages

HAWORTH Marriage and the Family
Terry S. Trepper, PhD
Executive Editor

Together Through Thick and Thin
A Multinational Picture of Long-Term Marriages

Shlomo A. Sharlin, PhD
Florence W. Kaslow, PhD
Helga Hammerschmidt, Dipl.Psych.

The Haworth Clinical Practice Press
An Imprint of The Haworth Press, Inc.
New York • London • Oxford

Published by

The Haworth Clinical Practice Press, an imprint of The Haworth Press, Inc., 10 Alice Street, Binghamton, NY 13904-1580

Acknowledgment
"On Marriage" from The Prophet by Kahlil Gibran. Copyright 1923 by Kahlil Gibran and renewed 1951 by Administrators C T A of Kahlil Gibran Estate and Mary G. Gibran. Reprinted by permission of Alfred A. Knopf, a division of Random House Inc.

Cover design by Monica L. Seifert.

Library of Congress Cataloging-in-Publication Data

Sharlin, Sh.
    Together through thick and thin : a multinational picture of long-term marriages / Shlomo A. Sharlin, Florence W. Kaslow, Helga Hammerschmidt.
        p.   cm.
    Includes bibliographical references and index.
    ISBN 0-7890-0492-5 (alk. paper) — ISBN 0-7890-0493-3 (pbk. : alk. paper)
        1. Marriage—Cross-cultural studies. 2. Married people—Psychology—Cross-cultural studies. 3. Satisfaction—Cross-cultural studies. 4. Family life surveys. I. Title: Multi-national picture of long-term marriages. II. Kaslow, Florence Whiteman. III. Hammerschmidt, Helga. IV. Title.

HQ728 .S47 2000
306.81—dc21
                                                                                                    99-462146

To our respective spouses, Solis Kaslow, Jost Hammerschmidt, and Nurit Sharlin, to whom we have each been married more than twenty-five years, and to the wonderful children of each of these long-term, satisfying marriages.

ABOUT THE AUTHORS

Shlomo A. Sharlin, PhD, is the founder and director of the Center for Research and Study of the Family in Haifa, Israel. He also serves as a consultant on family affairs to professional and government agencies, and teaches full time at the School of Social Welfare and Health Studies, University of Haifa. Dr. Sharlin is an international lecturer and consultant on family issues and family therapy. He has published several books and numerous articles on family issues.

Florence W. Kaslow, PhD, is in independent practice as a therapist, mediator, and family business consultant in West Palm Beach, Florida. She is also director of the Florida Couples and Family Institute, an Adjunct Professor of Medical Psychology at Duke University Medical School, and a Visiting Professor of Psychology at the Florida Institute of Technology. Dr. Kaslow has been teaching marital therapy for over 30 years, trying to help couples make their marriages both satisfying and long-lasting. She is a past editor of the *Journal of Marital and Family Therapy* and the author of several books.

Helga Hammerschmidt, MA, Dipl.Psych., is a psychologist and psychotherapist concentrating on couple and family research. She has lived and practiced in the United States and Latin America for over 15 years, acquiring comprehensive transcultural experience in family therapy and research. She currently practices and resides near Munich, Germany.

CONTENTS

Foreword

More than half a century ago, American political figure Wendell Willkie made the concept of "one world" a part of the international consciousness. Technological growth in quantum leaps and increasingly rapid and prevalent geographical mobility today starkly thrust upon us the impact of living on a shrinking globe in an expanding universe. The simultaneous shrinking of our planet and the expanding of awareness that we exist in infinite universes bring us closer together than ever before in human history. The result is not always benign intimacy.

It does not take an extraordinary amount of observation to ascertain that humankind faces the challenge of living together in reasonable understanding and tolerance or risks fragmentation into conflict under the stresses of greater closeness and rising anxiety. Politically, the breakdown of isolated tribalism can lead to wars of bullets and bombs or to cooperation and mutual advancement. Similarly, the crumbling of walls of professional isolation can result in bickering and jealousy or the nurturing of professional growth and advancement of beneficent services to those whom professionals claim to help.

The International Family Therapy Association (IFTA) was created in 1987 in response to the increasing manifestations of "one world" and the needs and opportunities of family therapists to act responsibly and in accordance with their professed high purpose and noble vision. The objectives of IFTA include: the advancement of family therapy as a science and method of treatment that regards the entire family as a unit; fostering international cooperation and interchange of ideas of those who are concerned with the needs of families and the practice of family therapy; dissemination of information to practitioners and others throughout the world; and the promotion of research and professional education, including the fostering of collaborative research projects across national boundaries.

Launched in 1992 by Florence Kaslow and reported here as *Together Through Thick and Thin: A Multinational Picture of Long-Term Marriages,* this is the first major research project completed by a group of IFTA scholars and clinicians. Shlomo A. Sharlin (Israel), Kaslow (United States), and Helga Hammerschmidt (Germany), the editors and guiding forces for the project, have brought together work from eight countries in North America (the United States and Canada), Western Europe (Germany, Sweden, and the Netherlands), South America (Chile), South Africa, and the Middle East (Israel). They explore a topic of growing interest as increasing segments of our populations live longer.

Where does this work belong in the family studies literature? The authors of this extensive study of long-term marriages clearly lay out the scope of their research and its methodological characteristics, strengths, and shortcomings. Those aspects of the material require little or no additional comment. Therefore, rather than focusing on the details of this multinational study, this foreword is directed to the larger meaning of the study.

Politically and practically, this work embodies a significant achievement of international cooperation. Both IFTA and the scholars involved in this extensive study can feel justifiable pride in an effort in which geographical distance, language, and other cultural differences were surmounted to produce a model for future collaborative research. Rather than relying on a single scholar or group of researchers to study marriages across cultures, in their own society and in others, this project took a different tack. Authors generally studied long-term marriages in their own societies, with the results then compared and summarized. Also, there were examples of collaborative research in which one of the editors worked with colleagues from another country on the colleague's study. Interestingly, the editors conclude: "Comparisons can be made between the countries, despite some sample differences, since the differences were found to be small and not very important" (p. 129). Although this finding might not prevail if studies of long-term marriages were included from other countries, Far Eastern for example, or from black, Asian, or Native American couples, it is still helpful to find this implicit support for Harry Stack Sullivan's "one genus postulate"—"that we are all more simply human than otherwise."

In a somewhat atypical action for those who are clinically concerned with problem populations, the authors involved in this study refreshingly focused on the salutogenic aspects of long-term marriages. "Salutogenic" is a research paradigm that incorporates research and theory on hardiness, resiliency, and learned resourcefulness. They look at success and positive functioning, and unlike most of the few predecessor studies on happy or healthy family life, which have concentrated on the early stages of family life, they examine these results in marriages which have lasted several decades. This study fits rather comfortably in the tradition of the work of Jerry Lewis, W. Robert Beavers, and colleagues, who contributed exceedingly helpful insights on psychological health and family systems a quarter century ago. This is a welcomed continuation of an often-neglected emphasis.

The authors' determination that the lack of need to compare the data from different countries according to sample characteristics not only is a major finding in itself but also lays the foundation for the conclusion that long-term satisfying marriage is a universal phenomenon. They note:

> It is inspiring to realize that perhaps the most important statistic is not that 20 to 50 percent of marriages end in divorce, depending on the country, but that 50 to 80 percent of marriages are long-lasting, with the majority of couples rating themselves as quite happy. (p. x)

The findings behind the authors' statement are available in the text for the reader to explore and digest on his or her own. There appear to be many couples who find long-lasting marriage enjoyable and satisfying.

Many of the men and women reporting on their marriages in this study fit into what American newscaster Tom Brokaw has described as "the greatest generation." They lived through the worldwide Great Depression of the early 1930s and survived the conflagration of World War II along with other major times of turmoil and stress. Such experiences certainly have the potential to squeeze hope, optimism, and belief in goodness and higher powers from human beings, but this does not appear to have occurred among these men and women who are engaging in successful long-term marriages.

Rather, for the majority of these couples, a religious affiliation and belief system derived from their religion provided an important foundation for their unwavering commitment to marriage. The recent emphasis on—or rediscovery of—spirituality by marital and family therapists appears to be consistent with some of the values held by the populace. What are the roles of spirituality and religious belief among those with whom the therapist and educator work?

The authors point out a few implications of their research for marital and family therapy. It is worth noting that their study not only tends to support the results of prior research with nonclinical populations but also is compatible with findings from work with couples in problematic marriages. From an examination of 100 consecutive marital cases of mine, first reported in 1978, I found that five practical constructs emerged: commitment, caring, communication, conflict and compromise, and "contract" (the combination of implicit and explicit expectations that the marital partners hold with regard to their marriage and spouse). The "five Cs" not only describe factors that are the loci of conflicts, but are also useful in building a workable and effective marital relationship. The conclusions from this multinational study generally are consistent with and expand my own intuitive and qualitative findings. Whether marriages are long term, short term, successful, or problematic, it appears that there are some common factors that figure in problematic or successful, happy outcomes.

Together Through Thick and Thin inevitably causes one to raise the intriguing and speculative question of what the picture will look like thirty-five to fifty years hence for those who are now in the early stages of marriage. The kind of multinational research reported here certainly needs to be continued and expanded. It has excellent potential for providing not only greater understanding of marriage—the central and lone voluntary family relationship for the majority of adults—but also for enabling marital and family therapists to be more knowledgeable and effective in working with couples and families in this increasingly complex world.

William C. Nichols, EdD, ABPP
President, International Family Therapy Association
(1999-2001)

Preface

Years of treating couples and families who are severely trauma-
tized by divorce, plus a long-standing interest in healthy individuals
and families, eventually led Florence Kaslow to conduct research
on long-term successful marriages—to garner a deeper understanding of what really leads to durable, healthy relationships rather than
to ones that become destructive, debilitating, and ultimately lead to
divorce. This venture also seemed like it would be a good antidote
to the infectious sadness one is vulnerable to when working with
couples whose dreams are terminating in a painful parting process.

Fortunately, a wonderful potential research associate happened
onto the scene in the person of Helga Hammerschmidt, a family
researcher from Munich, who was temporarily living in south Florida. She was also interested in this topic and joined Kaslow in
conducting and writing the initial pilot project. When Hammerschmidt returned to Germany, she asked to replicate the study there.
Kaslow became enthusiastic about the prospect of expanding the
database and obtaining cross-cultural data that would lend itself to
some interesting and potentially illuminating material. As other
colleagues heard about the project, they also asked to do replications in their countries. In particular, Kjell Hansson of Sweden;
Arturo Roizblatt of Chile; Shlomo Sharlin, of Israel; and Jacqueline
Meyerowitz of South Africa came on board as fellow researchers in
the mid-1990s and participated as presenters on various panels at
International Family Therapy Association (IFTA) conferences.
Sharlin became research coordinator for the project, while Kaslow
remained principal investigator. Later, Lore Finklestein of the Netherlands and Rina Cohen of Canada also asked to join the study
group, and the findings from these replications are included in the
total project represented in this book. A second phase of the U.S.
project was conducted with Jamie Robison, then a doctoral candi-
date serving as Kaslow's research assistant, and gratitude is ex-

tended to him as it is to all of the other research assistants and associates who participated in other countries. Special thanks are also extended to Victor Moin, who coordinated the international data analysis, and to Sharon Woodrow for her thorough editing. Last, but not least, our heartfelt thanks go out to Jeannette Solomon, without whose dedication, typing, and retyping this book would never have been possible. Our gratitude is also expressed to William Palmer at The Haworth Press, and Terry Trepper, Editor of the Family Therapy Book Program at Haworth, for their confidence in this project and in this book.

We believe this is the largest multinational, multicultural study of long-term marriages to be conducted to date. It includes separate data from couples in eight countries, as well as data that are combined and compared across different national samples. The results obtained concur with major findings from prior studies by others and go beyond these, adding not only multinational information and comparisons but other ingredients and motives that respondents indicate have been vital to them. It is inspiring to realize that perhaps the important statistic is not that 20 to 50 percent of marriages end in divorce, depending on the country, but that 50 to 80 percent of marriages are long-lasting, with the majority of couples rating themselves as quite happy. Hopefully, these data will enable therapists to have a profile in mind to help them assist the couples they treat in finding their way toward a more satisfying and contented spousal relationship.

This book consists of three parts, each focusing on a different aspect of our study. Part I deals with the background of the study. Chapter 1 presents an overview of the problem under investigation, mainly marriage and marital satisfaction. Chapter 2 summarizes theoretical issues and correlates of marital satisfaction. It includes a review of the literature on the issue of long-term marriages, as well as theoretical issues of marital quality and stability. Chapter 3 presents the methodology of our research. It covers such issues as sampling procedure and a detailed description of the instruments used for this cross-cultural study.

Part II includes a detailed report of the findings in each of the eight participating countries according to their continent. Chapter 4 reports on the studies conducted in North America, Chapter 5 focuses on Western Europe, and Chapter 6 reports on the findings from the other countries.

Part III presents the comparative analysis of the data from the eight countries. Chapter 7 compares the differences and similarities on a variety of issues, including those of ingredients for marital satisfaction and motives for staying together in long-term marriages. Chapter 8 deals with the implications of these findings for marital and family therapy and for couples who want to build long-term successful marriages.

PART I:
BACKGROUND OF THE STUDY

Chapter 1

Overview

The renowned Persian poet Kahlil Gibran (1923, pp. 15-16) says of marriage:

> Then Almitra spoke again and said, And what of Marriage, master?
> And he answered saying:
> You were born together, and together you shall be forevermore.
> You shall be together when the white wings of death scatter your days.
> Ay, you shall be together even in the silent memory of God.
> But let there be spaces in your togetherness,
> And let the winds of the heavens dance between you.
>
> Love one another, but make not a bond of love:
> Let it rather be a moving sea between the shores of your souls.
> Fill each other's cup but drink not from one cup.
> Give one another of your bread but eat not from the same loaf.
> Sing and dance together and be joyous, but let each one of you be alone,
> Even as the strings of a lute are alone though they quiver with the same music.
>
> Give your hearts, but not into each other's keeping.
> For only the hand of Life can contain your hearts.

Appreciation is expressed to Jacqueline B. Meyerowitz, a consultant to the Family Life Centre, Parkwood, Johannesburg, South Africa, who conducted the study portion done in South Africa, assisted by other members of the Family Life Centre, and for her contributions to this introductory chapter.

And stand together yet not too near together:
For pillars of the temple stand apart,
And the oak tree and the cypress grow not in each other's shadow.

Marriage has two important aspects. First, marriage is highly demanding and difficult to make satisfying, as is reflected in the high divorce rate in the Western world, and second, both single and divorced individuals seem strongly drawn toward marrying, the latter even if after disastrous experiences with earlier marriages. It appears, therefore, that the way in which some people seek marital status could have a compulsive quality. However, the particularly human needs for physical, emotional, and intellectual interchange, and more specifically the needs for intimacy and belonging, for affection and trust, and for the validation of experience, do not always find fulfillment within marriage.

At a time when in most Western countries the high divorce rate almost parallels the number of long-term marriages, it is important to understand the forces that hold marriages together. One way to acquire this information is to explore the quality of intact marriages, of stable marriages that are preserved by both partners. This focus is different from most previous approaches to understanding couple and family relationships, whereby studies seem to have been based on respondents seeking clinical help, on pathology, and on failed relationships. Although a great deal of research and numerous books and articles have dealt with divorce and its causes (Ahrons and Rogers, 1987; Gottman and Levenson, 1992; Kaslow, 1994; Schwartz and Kaslow, 1997), very few studies have researched lasting marriages and positive relationships by looking at their success. Learning from success means considering "positive functioning," how "normal" people overcome crises, and what coping mechanisms are used so successfully.

Most studies investigating the key factors of a happy or healthy marriage have concentrated on the early stages of family life (Kaslow, 1981, 1982; Lewis et al., 1976) and/or provided a general overview of "normal family processes" (Beavers, 1977, 1982; Walsh, 1982). The variables associated with satisfaction in marriages of long duration have not often been considered. Therefore, the goal of the pilot study, which was initiated by Kaslow (Kaslow and Hammerschmidt, 1992) in the United States, was to focus on long-term married couples who chose to stay together after their child-rearing and launching years were likely to be over, in order to determine the essential ingredients for such longevity.

This pilot project was later expanded in the United States (Kaslow and Robison, 1996) and replicated in Sweden (Kaslow, Hansson, and Lundblad, 1994). Similar research followed in Germany (Hammerschmidt and Kaslow, 1995), in Israel (Sharlin, 1996), in Chile (Roizblatt et al., 1999), in South Africa (Meyerowitz, 1996), in the Netherlands (Finkelstein, 1996), and most recently in Canada (Cohen, 1998).* The respondents participating in this research make up a nonclinical population of couples who have been married for a minimum of twenty years (except Sweden, where some were living together). This means that the data obtained from the eight countries came from a population group that was almost entirely over forty-five years of age, with some couples entering what is sometimes referred to as the "empty-nest" stage and possibly the first decade of retirement. Some, married up to the forty-five-year mark, were well into their sixties and seventies.

The studies were replicated using similar methodology, thereby contributing to cross-cultural and cross-national comparisons between the participating countries. This should lead to a greater understanding of what is unique in each country and what is universal in satisfying long-term marriages. Replications were not as exact as the authors had intended, given the necessity of translating the material into numerous different languages and making minor culturally relevant adaptations, which led to some small differences across studies.

The years from 1920 to 1945, when most of the partners in this research were born, and from 1945 to 1970, when most of the couples got married, included decades of enormous upheaval (World War II, the wars in Southeast Asia and in the Middle East)

---

*This was to become the first research project adapted by the research committee of the International Family Therapy Association (IFTA) and originally initiated by Florence Kaslow, founding president of IFTA. Project researchers are all IFTA members.

and unprecedented social, political, and technological changes. These changes included the women's movement and its consequences, as well as many scientific and technological advances, including the advent of television, cellular phones, and computers. The consequences of the foregoing have affected attitudes toward marriage, expectations of spousal roles and child-rearing practices, living conditions, and the subsequent possible need for renegotiation of the marital agreement, often a verbal one, during the various stages in a marriage.

This research project has concentrated on a time of life when perhaps for many couples in their middle and later years, marriage is central to, and an integral part of, their lives. Such a relationship is perceived as fundamental for a good quality of life and for optimal mental and physical health.

Specific aims of this international research project were:

- to determine the characteristics and components of successful marriages, which have enabled the spouses to sustain their relationships through the stresses and problems that inevitably arise during the course of the life stages of a marriage;
- to provide a broad picture of the varied ethnic, religious, cultural, and socioeconomic groups from which respondents were drawn and their possible influences on the couple;
- to explore the uniquenesses and differences inherent in long-term satisfying marriages; and
- to compare the findings derived from the research across different national population groups.

The results obtained from the research are based on a sample of 575 couples. The intent is to analyze and disseminate the information obtained from these respondents, in order to enable therapists and others working with troubled relationships to initiate interventions and to support couples who wish to stay together by improving their marital satisfaction for the benefit of themselves, their families, and ultimately for the community as a whole.

Additional factors explored by the various researchers were: differences between the perceptions and experiences of males and females in contributing to satisfying marriages (Finkelstein, 1996; Hammerschmidt and Kaslow, 1995; Sharlin, 1996); comparisons between the respondents and their parents' marriages (Roizblatt et al., 1999); whether all long-term marriages are successful and satisfying (Sharlin, 1996); what factors differentiate a more satisfying/happy marriage from a less satisfying/happy one (Finkelstein, 1996; Kaslow, Hansson, and Lundblad, 1994); the association between perceived happiness in childhood and marital satisfaction (Roizblatt et al., 1999); the association between SOC (sense of coherence) and marital satisfaction; and gender differences in SOC (Kaslow, Hansson, and Lundblad, 1994).

A marriage is a dynamic relationship that changes over time. Each spouse brings his or her beliefs, values, and expectations about marriage to the relationship. The couple's personal and subjective views of satisfaction, happiness, and marital health develop through their life experiences, family relationships, social contexts, economic situations, and personal attributes.

Satisfaction in marriage may differ in degree and in meaning. Various authors discuss satisfaction in marriage as a concept that implies a broad sense of fulfillment, well-being, contentment, and an overall good feeling, including a contented state of mind, camaraderie, affection, and safety (Wallerstein and Blakeslee, 1995). Satisfaction encompasses a sense of cooperation and mutual support, the feeling that there is a sincere and loving friendship, affection, fulfilling togetherness, and open, honest, tactful communication, which, in turn, encourages mutual understanding.

Some couples may prefer the safety of a marriage to living apart, for fear of loneliness, too much change, financial insecurity, or loss of status. Other, less satisfied couples, who manage to keep their marriages from irrevocably breaking down, may be influenced by parental pressures, by personal moral, ethical, or religious convictions, or by societal prescriptions and sanctions. They may be staying together for the sake of the children, rather than for reasons of personal commitment or mutual attraction. Willi (1991) offers the following as reasons why some couples stay together: habit, comfort, fears of being alone, anxieties about change and uncertainty, fear of losing social prestige and social security, as well as neurotic reasons.

Satisfaction may also be experienced differently according to the personal strengths of the partners during times of crisis, and in relation to the various stages and their accompanying transitions during marriage. The stresses of adjustment often begin with the birth of the first child, followed by possible pressures on women and the marriage during the child-rearing period in the early stages of marriage. Other transitional stages include when children leave home; menopause; retirement, which can bring loss of status, role, and income; and the loss of parents. The advent of illness in the family may lead to one of the partners becoming the dominant caregiver, which could be seen as a marital imbalance by an outsider, but may be acceptable to the couple concerned.

It is the appearance of unresolved issues during the middle years, when a couple is faced with many changes in roles, to which those in the helping professions are attuned. Difficulties tend to escalate for dissatisfied couples, and although a growing number of couples are seeking divorce after twenty years of marriage, there are also couples who persist in an unsatisfying relationship with a sense of resignation and sadness.

It is suggested that couples experiencing a solid and fulfilling relationship have better resources for coping with the strains of life, and that the stability of a modern marriage depends more upon the level of satisfaction than was the case in former decades. It appears, then, that for most couples who choose to remain married, the quality of their relationship greatly influences their happiness and satisfaction. Like the poem by Gibran, the commitment to the ideal "together you shall be forever more" is reflected in this research as a commitment to the permanency of the relationship.

Sharlin (1996, p. 225) refers to several studies in which it has been shown that marital satisfaction is a key variable in predicting the length of marriages (Spanier, 1976; Greeley, 1981; Schlesinger, 1982; Schlesinger and Schlesinger, 1987; Kaslow, 1981, 1982; Fields, 1983; Fennell, 1987; Fincham, 1991). Roizblatt and colleagues (1999) refer to Luckey (1964), who found that husbands and wives indicating higher satisfaction with their marriages were those whose perceptions were in greater agreement with each other. They also cite Lauer and Lauer (1986), who examined 351 couples in mainly long-term marriages and found that the two most notable factors identified by those perceived as happily married were friendship and liking each other.

The feeling of happiness in a marriage correlates with success, prosperity, good fortune, and a sense of gratification arising from one's circumstances or conditions. In general, the majority of people agree that sufficient money, success at work, and good health are of major importance in marital contentment. Nonetheless, some couples in the lower and middle socioeconomic ranges are content in their marriages, feel good about themselves and what they have accomplished, and do not measure happiness in materialistic terms. One of the basic aspects of well-being for both partners is the ability to relate satisfactorily, and to achieve this, there needs to be a great deal of mutual trust. A happy marriage reflects a shared perception of the essence of trust and closeness so that the resulting intimacy leads to "a special goodness of fit between their individual needs, wishes, and expectations, which enables them both to feel cherished, respected and in many instances, passionately loved throughout their adult lives" (Wallerstein, quoted in Roizblatt et al., 1999, p. 115).

Several unique features are characteristic of couples in only some of the countries included in this international research project. In Israel, the study included people who have emigrated from 112 countries and who have different cultural, ethnic, and national backgrounds. The respondents included a group of Holocaust survivors. In reporting on this part of the study, Sharlin (1996) pointed out that Israel has the lowest divorce rate in the West, attributable partially to the fact that family life is a highly valued norm among the Jewish people. The comparison of motives and ingredients for satisfying marriages in Israel and the other countries may therefore yield interesting results.

Meyerowitz (1996) notes the diversity of the South African population, colorfully described by President Mandela in 1994 as "The Rainbow People of South Africa." Although South Africa is reputed to have one of the highest divorce rates in the Western world, available statistics do not represent the whole population due to the fact that various cultural groups conduct and record marriages and divorces outside the jurisdiction of the civil court system. Another factor impinging on marriages in South Africa was the apartheid system of government, which was a fact of life over several decades and which led to much family disruption and hardship. Consequences of apartheid have included the weakening of traditional family values, often an absence of parental influence, and at times role confusion between family members.

In Sweden, most couples who eventually get married have lived together before the wedding, and fewer than five new marriages per 1,000 inhabitants take place every year (Kaslow, Hansson, and Lundblad, 1994). The researchers point out that although approximately 40,000 couples get married each year in Sweden, which they observe is a low figure compared to rates in the 1950s and 1960s, 80,000 to 90,000 new families are established each year. The high number of new families, in spite of the low number of new marriages, highlights the fact that eight out of nine new families are "just" living together, although many of these relationships lead to marriage.

Roizblatt et al. (1999) draws attention to the fact that the majority of couples in Chile follow the same religion and that their strong belief in Catholicism influences their marital bond. In the Dutch study, Finkelstein (1996) offers an insight into the personality of people in the Netherlands who have experienced the strong psychic impact of World War II and the postwar years, and have nevertheless succeeded in maintaining marital togetherness and in adapting to a world quite different from the one of their youth.

Mental health professionals are interested in what makes a marriage last, as this knowledge can provide useful information about how to help couples who are having difficulties and who wish to continue and improve their marriages. A pathogenic point of view, which is the most common one, tries to explain why people get "sick," divorce, or experience difficulties in resolving problems. A *salutogenic* perspective (Antonovsky, 1988) asks instead, What is it that makes some people cope and stay healthy, even though they are confronted with the same stresses and strains as those who become "sick" or get divorced? The focus adopted by this study of long-term satisfying marriages is salutogenic. In this respect, as viewed by Kaslow and Robison (1996) and the other researchers involved in this study, there is an assumption that couples who have spent twenty years and more together have a cluster of characteristics and attributes which have enabled them to manage the many different and difficult situations that have arisen in the course of their shared lives.

Although many different cultures and socioeconomic groups are represented in the total sample, several common threads can be extracted in exploring the quality of these marriages. For the most part, the respondents indicated having reasonable or good relationships with their own parents, having happy or fairly happy childhoods, and sharing common religious beliefs with one another despite not always practicing their religion. Willi (1991) states that people with similar backgrounds are more likely to have similar constructs and that it has been statistically documented that most individuals seek homogamy in their choice of mate, that is, an agreement in cultural, religious, and other background factors, in tastes, and in intellectual interests.

The structure provided by parents of the respondents, who were themselves in most cases married for over thirty years, contributed to a sense of stability, order, and belonging, and this may explain why the majority of couples in the sample chose "marriage is a partnership for life" as the most important motive for staying married. There is an intergenerational transmission of the importance of commitment to marriage and the family and therefore to family continuity. Likewise, Wallerstein and Blakeslee (1995) describe a good marriage as a unit that shapes adults and children and as such "more than any other human institution, is a vehicle for transmitting . . . values to future generations" (p. 337).

It is possible that the parents and the respondents share some salient common characteristics, particularly in the "differentiation of self" within the family of origin (Bowen, 1976, pp. 65-89). The more differentiated the individual, the more freedom from internal anxiety one has and the more flexible and adaptable to external stimuli one can be. Bowen believed that the level of differentiation of an individual is largely determined by the time he or she leaves the family or origin and attempts a life of his or her own. He also contends that such an individual tends to replicate the parents' lifestyle in all subsequent relationships. Bowen describes marriage as a "functioning partnership"; thus, if and when individuals at lower levels of differentiation marry, the potential for future problems and dissatisfaction in the marriage is greater. When more

emotionally differentiated individuals marry, they are likely to select partners who are on a level of emotional development similar to
their own. In this study, it is postulated that individuals who have
maintained mutually satisfying long-term marriages have each
reached a similar level of emotionally healthy and mature development. As Kaslow and Hammerschmidt observe (1992), "It is from
the unions of two healthy, high well-being adults that healthy families evolve" (p. 19).

In this research project, a small percentage of couples had experienced unhappy childhoods and conflict with one or both parents. A
few participants had divorced and were in long-term second marriages. These factors may relate to replicating some parental themes
or to lower differentiation of self. However, in view of some unique
features discussed by authors from several countries (Finkelstein,
1996; Meyerowitz, 1996; Sharlin, 1996), an additional dimension
for future research may be to explore how couples and families
have adapted to traumatic events over time, particularly if families
and couples have faced enforced exile, war, or victimization. To
what extent have dissatisfied couples, married for twenty years and
more, inherited themes relating to traumatic events from the past,
such as the Holocaust or other genocides of political repression,
persecution, and slaughter (Kaslow, 1995, 1997)?

Notwithstanding the cultural and economic differences between
the respondents in the countries included in this study, several common ingredients for long-term satisfying marriages emerged. Both
men and women, with slight variation, emphasized the interactive
nature of the essential ingredients of a satisfying marriage. The
importance of mutuality was indicated repeatedly by the respondents' predominant choices of mutual trust, mutual respect, love,
mutual give-and-take, comradeship, interest in children, shared values and interests, and joint decision making. These results appear to
correspond with Fennell's (1987) and Murstein's (1980) research,
as discussed by Roizblatt et al. (1999). Fennell conducted a study of
147 couples in first marriages that had lasted over twenty years. His
major finding was that husbands and wives in satisfying marriages
expressed high levels of agreement regarding the important characteristics contributing to their long-term unions. Similarly, Murstein

found that the partners in successful marriages possess value consensus and role congruence.

In addition, Sharlin's (1996) results confirm the basic characteristics believed to account for satisfying and lasting marriages: similarity and congruence of background, including religion, education, lifestyle, and philosophy of life; living in the present and future rather than being stuck in the past; and an intrinsic motivation to make theirs a good and lasting relationship as the basis of marriage. As Gibran stated in the verse which opens this chapter: "sing and dance together and be joyous," so too did Kaslow and Hammerschmidt (1992) and Kaslow and Robison (1996) find that satisfied couples play well together and treasure the fun that they share.

The overall importance of this research is therefore to highlight those qualities of marriage which are positive, which have benefited couples, and which couples value. These qualities are important for those working with unhappy couples in order to discover possible untapped potentials that have been hidden or overwhelmed by an individual's or couple's negative feelings and behavior patterns over time.

It was assumed at the inception of each part of this study that couples who have spent twenty-plus years together have a group of qualities that make them able to cope with many different and difficult situations in the course of their shared lives. This research offers some validated data regarding which factors are most salient in this respect, namely factors that create more rather than less contented durable relationships. The remainder of the book presents a more in-depth analysis of the study population, methodology, and interpretation of results.

Chapter 2

Theoretical Underpinnings

Marital success involves marital stability and high quality (Glenn, 1990), which are separate and distinct dimensions (Lewis and Spanier, 1979). Marriages may endure or dissolve regardless of the level of quality (and quality may vary during the course of a relationship); nevertheless, the likelihood of stability grows with the improvement of quality.

The concept of *dyadic adjustment* or *dyadic quality* is defined as a comprehensive, subjective rating of the couple relationship (Spanier, 1976). Since our objective was to analyze cross-cultural and cross-national similarities and differences in long-term marriages, we selected marital satisfaction as the primary outcome variable being studied, with the multidimensional approach as a secondary concern. We concur that "marital satisfaction reflects the mood and happiness with regard to the overall functioning of marriage" (Olson, 1988, p. 73).

The expectations and desires of each spouse in marriage are pivotal. In addition, the agreement of the couple about what constitutes happiness for them is vital. Satisfaction entails having one's fundamental needs and desires met, as well as fulfilling the spouse's expectations. This means that couple satisfaction necessarily includes intradyadic as well as individual aspects. Consequently, one must consider the perception of both spouses for the assessment of marital success. Satisfaction implies a sense of well-being, contentment, and overall good feeling. For example, as has been shown in comprehensive psychoneuroimmunological research (Olson, 1996, p. 79), satisfied people are healthier.

Such a definition of satisfaction is broad enough to permit multicultural comparisons and to be applicable to all kinds of "mixed marriages." A narrow definition is not acceptable since different couples perceive satisfaction in quite different ways and require different levels of relational depth to achieve this. Although the two concepts of quality and satisfaction are generally highly correlated, it is necessary to differentiate them clearly, especially in multicultural, multinational research.

REVIEW OF LITERATURE AND EARLIER FINDINGS

Over sixty years ago, Terman et al. (1938) reported on the first important empirical study based upon research on more than 1,000 couples. After this pioneering research project, it was a long time until the topic of marital stability and quality surfaced again.

In the 1970s, some investigations were conducted that focused on marital satisfaction throughout the family life cycle. This research consistently suggested a curvilinear pattern with satisfaction at its lowest point when children were growing up (Burr, 1970; Rollins and Feldman, 1970; Rollins and Cannon, 1974). These studies paid more attention to the course of satisfaction over time than to the reasons for change in level of satisfaction. Later studies showed that marital satisfaction had to be seen in a more differentiated way. Changes in satisfaction are not only created by life events themselves; they also must be viewed in the context of circumstances, changes within the individual, and couple resources. Furthermore, the observed improvement in marital satisfaction over the course of years is also the result of a periodic selection process, in that at least some of the dissatisfied couples have parted while the more satisfied couples remained together.

Research on couple satisfaction, which takes into consideration stressors and resources, follows two distinct directions. They are best described by the following questions: "Why do marriages fail?" and "Why do marriages succeed?" According to the cross-sectional approach, followed in the majority of research studies, results have the character of a snapshot. The level of satisfaction at the time data is collected expresses to what extent mutual expectations have been fulfilled in regard to the relationship up to that moment. Since relationships have to be seen as process of development, the history of the whole couplehood is relevant to its success. Therefore, a longitudinal view is more appropriate. However, in cases of long-term developments, retrospective data, cohort studies, or short-term longitudinal investigation may serve as substitutes because of the difficulties inherent in this method of research.

CORRELATES OF MARITAL SATISFACTION

Good problem solving and good communication skills have been found consistently to be key factors for marital satisfaction (Ting-Toomey, 1982; Kaslow, 1982; Barnes et al., 1984; Hahlweg, Revenstorf, and Schindler, 1984; Olson, 1988; Kaslow and Hammerschmidt, 1992; Kaslow, Hansson, and Lundblad, 1994; Storaasli and Markman, 1990; Markman and Hahlweg, 1993; Gottman, 1994; Hammerschmidt and Kaslow, 1995; Sharlin, 1996). Furthermore, the following couple resources have been identified as pivotal: presence of self-disclosure (Hendrick, 1981; Hansen and Schuldt, 1984), shared value system (Murstein, 1980; Beavers, 1985), role congruence (Murstein, 1980), sensitivity to the feelings of and positive regard for the spouse (Barnes et al., 1984), the expectation and perception of reciprocity in positive behavioral exchanges (Jacobson and Margolin, 1979), the perception of an equal distribution of power in the marriage along with equal contributions to the marriage (Jacobson and Margolin, 1979; Beavers, 1985), the presence of children in the marriage (Luckey and Bain, 1970), shared interests (Schwarzenauer, 1980), and mutual support and dyadic coorientation in personal developmental perspectives regarding different behavioral areas and goal domains of development (Brandstädter, Baltes-Goetz, and Heil, 1990).

Conversely, negative interaction patterns are much more common in the lives of unhappily married couples (Margolin and Wampold, 1981; Ting-Toomey, 1982; Levenson and Gottman, 1983; Hahlweg, Revenstorf, and Schindler, 1984; Revenstorf et al., 1985). The key word here is "pattern," which implies the repetitive nature of exchanges. Indeed, during times of spousal disagreement, positive verbal behavior and compliance expressed by one spouse (generally the wife) may be functional in the short run. Although the couple's overall communication pattern needs to be positive, there must be a willingness to accept the expression of disagreement. Gottman and Krokoff (1989) found that for both members of the couple, the articulation of conflicting ideas and feelings reflected current marital dissatisfaction, yet was a predictor of probable improvement in satisfaction over time (providing the expression of disagreement led toward greater understanding and resolution and did not result in behaviors characterized by defensiveness, stubbornness, and withdrawal, particularly by husbands). Indeed, if a couple wish their union to be long-lasting and satisfying, they must develop confidence in their ability to weather conflict together. Notarius and Vancetti (1983) call this "relational efficacy."

Retrospective studies investigating separated and divorced individuals also speak to the issue of marital satisfaction, but from the opposite perspective. The individuals questioned by Bloom and Hodges (1981) identified two predominant factors in their marital dissatisfaction: communication difficulties and a lack of love. When responding to the question "What contributes most to your marital dissatisfaction?" Kayser's (1993) group of divorced or separated respondents reported actions by their partners that they perceived as being controlling and/or lacking in intimacy, or exhibiting negative behavioral traits, including the partner's inability to resolve problems, and differences in the lifestyles sought by each.

RESEARCH ON LONG-TERM MARRIAGES

Long-term marriages have been conceptualized herein as marriages that have lasted at least twenty years. Therefore, it is a good tool with which to study both dimensions—quality and stability—within the process of couple development. Consideration of the different courses relationships take, the periods of happiness, and crises in the context of strains and resources allows the discovery of how people succeed in creating fulfilling relationships. Different approaches can be utilized, including retrospective studies, cross-sectional studies, short-term longitudinal studies, and combinations of these approaches. Moreover, several methodologies can be utilized concurrently, including interviews, standardized questionnaires, and observation, which may be videotaped.

In their article "Half Century of Marriage: Continuity or Change?," Weishaus and Field (1988) describe six types of long-term marriages:

1. *Stable/positive:* These couples have maintained moderately high to high satisfaction and positive affect throughout their marriage.
2. *Stable/neutral:* This type describes couples that married for various reasons and never experienced high affect, though they still express overall satisfaction.
3. *Stable/negative:* Negative affect characterizes these marriages almost from their beginning.
4. *Curvilinear:* The satisfaction of these couples declined during the earlier stages, but was followed by an increase in the later stages.
5. *Continuous decline:* These couples began their marriage with moderately high to high levels of satisfaction but have experienced a continuous decrease.
6. *Continuous increase:* This phenomenon has been described for some arranged marriages. In the contemporary Western world, it would be unusual to find this type of continuous increase.

The sample for their study came from the longitudinal Berkley Older Generation Study, which yielded case records of seventeen marriages of fifty to sixty-nine years' duration. Data were collected at four life stages through interviews and observation.

Based on a study of 147 couples in first marriages lasting over twenty years, Fennell (1987) derived the following characteristics, which showed the greatest frequency:

- Lifetime commitment to marriage
- Respect for one's spouse as a best friend
- Loyalty to spouse and the expectation of reciprocity
- Mutual self-disclosure
- Strong, shared moral values
- Commitment to sexual fidelity
- Desire to be a good parent
- Faith in God and spiritual commitment
- Companionship with spouse, including spending a great deal of enjoyable time together over the course of a lifetime

Lauer, Lauer, and Kerr (1990) gathered data from 100 mainly upper-middle-class couples married from forty-five to sixty-five years. The variables identified as important were:

- Being married to partners they liked as people and enjoyed being with
- Commitment to the spouse and to marriage
- A sense of humor
- Consensus on various matters such as aims and goals in life, friends, and decision making

Notarius and Markman (1993) reported in *We Can Work It Out— Making Sense of Marital Conflict* the final results of their longitudinal investigation. For twenty years, they had conducted studies to identify the precise factors that determine successful marriages. Over twenty articles were published during this period of investigation (see, for example, Gottman et al., 1976; Hahlweg and Markman, 1988; Markman et al., 1991). The research involved diverse groups of happy and unhappy couples at all stages of the life cycle, from those planning to get married to those looking back on thirty-plus years of marriage and from a variety of ethnic backgrounds and socioeconomic classes. Each couple was interviewed, completed a series of questionnaires, and was videotaped discussing their most intense relationship issues. On the basis of the huge quantity of data collected, the researchers developed clinically proven methods to guide couples toward success and away from typical pitfalls. The Premarital Relationship Enhancement Program (PREP) was adapted in cooperation with researchers from different countries and has been used successfully for years. Several publications resulting from these efforts were written by Revenstorf et al. (1985), Hahlweg and Markman (1988), and Markman and Hahlweg (1993).

Gottman's (1994) book *Why Marriages Succeed or Fail* is also based on twenty years of research in which he observed and interviewed hundreds of couples and found three styles of stable marriages: the validating, the avoidant, and the volatile. He notes that some types of marriage require more work in certain areas than others because they face different risks. His so-called "four horsemen of the Apocalypse" are the four warning signs in troubled relationships: *criticism*, *contempt*, *defensiveness*, and *stonewalling*.

Among the key strategies Gottman identified for improving a marriage is agreeing with one's spouse on which style to use for handling disagreements; it should be one with which both can live and should include a large dose of "positivity." Case examples illustrate how to succeed in this process.

In *The Good Marriage: How and Why Love Lasts,* Wallerstein and Blakeslee (1995) reported the results of their study with fifty couples "happily married" from ten to forty years. The participants were interviewed, first separately and then together. The authors classify four basic types of marriage: *romantic, rescue, companionate,* and *traditional.* The natural stages of marriage are described and nine psychological tasks elucidated that should be fulfilled in order to have a satisfying relationship. The results of this study are portrayed in comprehensive dialogues of the participants.

In his book *Was Hält Paare Zusammen?* (What Keeps Couples Together?), Willi (1991) described the process of enduring relationships from his psychoecological view, based on case studies. He investigated the process of individual and intradyadic development in enduring relationships exploring the complexities and mysteries of love over the entire life span. On one hand, he reveals the secrets of couples in fulfilling relationships. On the other, he devotes special attention to those who experience their relationship as meaningful despite dissatisfaction. From his systemic view, he considers marital conflicts as interrupted or failed endeavors for development and growth. Consequently, he pronounces that those couples experience their joint life in different ways and explains that by accepting "des Getrenntbleibens in der Liebe" (self-reliance in love), they can gain an essential attitude that enables each to understand the other and to complement and broaden their own view through the views of their spouses.

In her book *Leidenschaft und Lange Weile* (Long-Lasting Passion), Welter-Enderlin (1992) published a summation based on comprehensive interviews with thirty-six couples who had consulted her during a crisis in the previous year. In addition to providing her with detailed knowledge of the history of the relationships prior to crisis intervention, this approach allowed her to follow the development of the relationships after therapy. Eighty percent of the couples interviewed stayed together. They explained what was helpful to them and which problems remained unresolved. The author shows how people can change their individual lives and their relationships instead of persisting in dissatisfaction. In her therapeutic approach, Welter-Enderlin considers, in addition to the individual biography and the history of the relationship, the resources and difficulties of the families of origin as well as the psychoecological and sociological context.

RESULTS OF THE PILOT STUDY FOR THIS PROJECT

A different focus was taken in the international study initiated and coordinated by Kaslow. During 1990-1991, Kaslow and Hammerschmidt (1992) conducted a pilot study. As reported in "Long-Term 'Good' Marriages: The Seemingly Essential Ingredients," this investigation was an attempt to determine the essential ingredients of longevity in marital relationships by analyzing questionnaire data derived from a study population of twenty couples. The questionnaire, which was constructed specifically for this study, included open-ended questions to ascertain to what the couples attributed their satisfaction and longevity. All of the couples had been married between twenty-five and forty-six years. Nineteen couples had had children; only four couples still had children living at home. The women ranged in age from forty-nine to seventy-one years, with a mean of fifty-nine years; the men ranged from forty-nine to seventy-four years of age, with a mean of sixty-two years. In terms of educational background, everyone had completed high school and all but three women and two men had gone on to higher education. Only one couple had already retired. In the other nineteen couples, all of the men and eighteen of the women were gainfully employed. The vast majority of the couples were Jewish, and their incomes placed them in the upper-middle to upper socioeconomic strata. In addition to the open-ended questions, several specially designed instruments and the Dyadic Adjustment Scale (Spanier, 1976) were used to elicit respondents' ideas as to what made their marriages work. The twenty respondent couples were ranked, and their responses were divided into three categories:

1. Very satisfied   10 couples
2. Midrange   6 couples
3. Dissatisfied   4 couples

In comparing the three groups, the following differences in the variables attributed to the longevity of marriage were found:

- Love, mutual respect and trust, shared interests and value systems, shared love for children, the ability to give and take, and flexibility were all mentioned much more frequently by satisfied couples, less so by midrange, and the least by dissatisfied couples.
- Sensitivity to the needs of one's spouse appears only in the satisfied group. An egalitarian relationship with many complementary features was also cited as important by satisfied couples, but less frequently than the factors mentioned previously.
- Interestingly, having and sharing an interest in their children was relayed by all as important in their lives together, but only by dissatisfied couples as a reason for the longevity of their marriage. The satisfied couples stayed together because they wanted to be with each other, and not primarily for the sake of their children. The dissatisfied couples also disclosed that they experienced a lack of affectional expressiveness and support from each other.
- The midrange couples revealed a deficit in the arena of good communication. Fun, humor, and playfulness rarely appear as factors in the responses of the midrange and dissatisfied couples, indicating that these are not a vital part of their lives together. In contrast, many of the satisfied couples stated that they savor having fun together.
- A strong sense of self is cited only in the midrange group as an important factor contributing to the longevity of their marriages.
- For the two variables of good sexual relationship and the availability of privacy and personal space when desired (Gibran also spoke of "spaces in the togetherness" as significant in marriage), few differences emerged among the three groups. Good joint problem-solving ability turned out to be the item

ranked as the key and major factor contributing to satisfaction for all respondents, even for most of the dissatisfied.

The question "To what factors do you attribute the longevity of your marriage?" was presented in an open-ended form. Significantly, the satisfied couples provided the greatest number of responses to this crucial question:

- Satisfied   7.25 answers per person (mean)
- Mid-range   5.12 answers per person (mean)
- Unsatisfied   3.75 answers per person (mean)

This can be interpreted as a reflection of the satisfied individuals' greater awareness of what is conducive to their happiness and of an appreciation of the emotional richness of their lives. Conversely, the paucity of responses of the dissatisfied couples represents their constricted relationships and overall discontent.

Furthermore, study respondents were asked what advice they would give to others to help them achieve satisfying relationships. Since wise advice can be derived as much from positive as from negative experience, we combined the responses from the three categories of subjects as follows:

1. Give and take, compromise.
2. Establish and maintain good communication.
3. Respect your spouse and treat him or her as an equal.
4. Establish a tight (close and cohesive) family.
5. Be supportive of your spouse.
6. Be sensitive to and considerate of the needs of your spouse.
7. Trust each other; be honest.
8. Maintain a balance between individuality and couplehood.
9. Love each other and be committed to the relationship.
10. Have fun together as often as possible.
11. Marry someone with similar values, or develop these together.
12. Share interests and activities so time together is well spent.
13. Choose a partner with a similar background.
14. Work together for financial security.
15. Be affectionate; stay in touch sensually.
16. Solve problems as they arise.

Healthy, high-functioning individuals are the most apt to be attracted to a partner who is also self-actualizing and has a good self-image, yet is able to be considerate of, sensitive to, and capable of commitment to a significant other. Such pairings seem to produce the kind of long-term marital satisfaction that was addressed in this research.

Prior to this study, most of the research on later-life couples had been conducted in the United States, Canada, and the U.K. The intent of this larger, more inclusive study was to go beyond these three countries to provide a more multiethnic, multicultural, and multireligious portrait of couples across the socioeconomic spectrum, detailing the essential ingredients of long-term successful marriages. The study included the self-perceptions of the respondent couples and the combined analysis and interpretation of the data from eight countries on five different continents.

UNDERLYING THEORETICAL APPROACH

To study long-term marriages, it appeared essential to focus our investigation on the determinants of marital stability as well as of marital quality. Our goal was to select relevant variables that fit together to form a coherent model. The selection of these variables was based on the composite results of previous investigations as well as on observations derived from our own couple therapy. Our model attempts to bridge research, theory, and practice.

The *theory of marital quality and marital stability* (Lewis and Spanier, 1979), which is based on exchange theory assumptions, stands in an overarching position integrating all components we considered relevant. The *Circumplex* and/or *MASH Model* (Multisystem Assessment of Stress and Health) (Olson and Stewart, 1990) served as a conceptual framework for exploring the importance and interplay of resources in the exchange process. The influence of variables related to childhood and family of origin can be considered not only from a psychodynamic viewpoint but also from a perspective based on assumptions about modeling behavior (Bandura, 1977).

Although we did not collect any specific information regarding mate selection, this topic cannot be ignored in the discussion of marital success, since the choice of mate has a basic influence on the later development of the relationship. There exists a great variety of theoretical approaches in reference to mate selection, including:

- Theory of complementary needs (Winch, 1958);
- Filter theory (Kerckhoff and Davis, 1962);
- Stimulus-value comparison-role theory (Murstein, 1970); and
- Mate selection as an interpersonal process (Huston and Levinger, 1978).

The psychodynamic approach posits that mate selection is influenced by unconscious needs and occurs in a complementary way. Willi (1975/1990) uses the core concept of "collusion" to refer to the unconscious interplay between spouses based on similar, unresolved central conflicts. He perceives a couple's relationship as a system in which the spouses' behaviors are determined both by personal history and their interdependence. Using a psychodynamic framework, he stresses that both parties hope to overcome past traumas and conflicts through what they derive from the marital interaction. In their joint defense alliance, they both enhance their partnership by polarizing into complementary roles: One mate seeks resolution through progressive behavior; the other through regressive behavior. When their defense alliance collapses, which it almost always does, the disillusionment precipitates serious marital crises.

Emotionally healthy individuals are apt (perhaps even destined) to gravitate toward and select another healthy person at the same level of individuation from the family of origin (Bowen, 1988). It is from the union of two healthy, well-adjusted adults that healthy families evolve. Consequently, our study explored premarital factors that were hypothesized to influence marital quality. Although the investigation was concentrated on couple interaction, other considerations included personal resources and socioeconomic and sociocultural context factors.

Exchange theory (Kelley, 1983) generally postulates that social interaction depends on the exchange of material and immaterial values. In the exchange process in relationships, each partner maintains certain goals in and provides certain resources to the relationship. Interactions are realized and gain stability if the partners assume and experience relative advantages. In marital relationships, resources take on an especially emotional nature. Kelley further posited that the level of marital quality experienced is compared to perceived alternatives and that the attraction of a relationship depends on the degree of positive comparison. Commitment to marriage is reinforced through attraction and satisfaction with the relationship and grows in accordance with the investment of time and resources.

Theory of Marital Quality and Marital Stability

Lewis and Spanier (1979) formulated the following three basic propositions:

1. The greater the social and personal resources available for adequate marital role functioning, the higher the subsequent marital quality.
2. The greater the spouses' satisfaction with their lifestyle, the greater their marital quality.
3. The greater the rewards from spousal interaction, the greater the marital quality.

As a consequence of the observation that independent of the level of marital quality, some couples separate and others do not, Lewis and Spanier expanded their model to explain the observed discrepancy between quality and stability: "Although marital quality and stability are highly correlated, it is likely that threshold variables operate as forces which allow some couples to pass over the threshold and separate while not allowing others to pass" (Lewis and Spanier, 1979, p. 285). They concluded from this assumption that there are four combinations of quality and stability (see Table 2.1).

Lewis and Spanier emphasize that "the model is necessarily oversimplified in that we assume an arbitrary dichotomy between high and low marital quality, but this is of consequence only insofar as it is important to know the precise point where a couple might have moved from one quadrant to another. A more complex model would provide for a nonstationary vertical axis, or multiple vertical axes to allow for more gradations of marital quality" (1979, p. 287).

TABLE 2.1. Typology of Marital Quality and Marital Stability

S **T** **A** **B**	High stability IV Low quality	High stability I High quality
I **L** **I** **T** **Y**	Low stability III Low quality	Low stability II High quality

↑
Y   X →   QUALITY

Source: Adapted from Lewis and Spanier, 1979.

The horizontal axis refers to factors that influence marital quality. Primarily, these variables function on the intradyadic level:

- Couple resources: closeness, flexibility, communication, problem solving (Health and Stress Profile, Olson and Stewart, 1990, 1991); consensus, affectional expression, cohesion (Dyadic Adjustment Scale, Spanier, 1976)
- Ingredients such as mutual trust, appreciation, respect, give and take, support, loyalty and fidelity, sensitivity and consideration for needs of spouse

Some other intrapersonal variables should be added here:

- Individual resources: e.g., fairness, reliability, being patient and understanding
- Values and beliefs that function as resources in direct or indirect ways in the coping process

The vertical axis refers to variables affecting marital stability. They were previously referred to as threshold variables. These factors, which mitigate against separation, are as follows:

- Social norms and expectations
- Importance of religious conviction

- Commitment to the relationship
- Values and beliefs that function as a barrier against divorce without influencing marital quality

Thus, we have differentiated between two major categories in our analysis of motives that are conducive to marital stability:

One category consists of motives that express marital satisfaction and consequently have been related to the horizontal axis of the model:

- Intrinsic motivation provides the most vital power in happy relationships. It includes partner-related motives as well as partnership-related motives: Partner-related motives are exclusively related to the partner as a person per se and meet the spouses' healthy needs; partnership-related motives are those which represent the continuing process of give and take, as well as connectedness.
- Positive problem solving involves the attitude and ability to do so as an essential couple resource.
- Extrinsic motivation results from the consideration of economic, practical, or social advantages that the relationship offers. Disadvantages reduce the valence of attraction.

The other category of motives includes those which influence stability without contributing to quality:

- Social norms and expectations as well as outside pressure
- Commitment to marriage or values without influence on quality
- Neurotic motives, including dependency, lack of self-esteem, and in extreme cases, severe pathology

Low degrees of threshold variables, as well as a high attraction of extramarital alternatives, raise the probability of divorce. The influence of extramarital attraction on the level of stability was not considered in this study, but certainly plays a disruptive role in some marriages. During crisis situations, when conflict, tension, and dissatisfaction grow, the strength of barriers against extramarital affairs will influence the degree of continuing marital stability. Thus, we assessed the motives for marital stability that had proven to be crucial during the most difficult stages of the marriage. Lewis and Spanier (1979) emphasized "that a couple may move from one point within a quadrant [see Table 2.1] to another or to different points within a given quadrant over time, depending on the balance between the positive and negative intradyadic factors and the balance of extradyadic factors" (p. 287).

The major propositions of the theory of marital quality and stability are:

1. The better the marital quality, the greater the marital stability.
2. Alternative attractions to a marriage negatively influence the strength of the relationship between quality and stability.
3. External pressures to remain married positively influence the strength of the relationship between quality and stability.

Figure 2.1 depicts the theory of marital quality and stability, as developed by Lewis and Spanier (1979, p. 289) and adapted to our study.

The MASH Model and the Circumplex Model

This investigation is focused mainly on the intradyadic situation and partially interpreted in light of the Circumplex and/or MASH Model (Olson and Stewart, 1991). The MASH Model follows Antonovsky's (1988) salutogenic approach and combines elements of previous family and individual stress research. The MASH Model is designed to be used with nonclinical populations, as suggested in the salutogenic approach, which is particularly relevant to this study.

Antonovsky recommended that instead of studying the symptoms of disease, one should focus the investigation on the symptoms of wellness. He suggested that coping variables need to be abstracted one step higher in order to find "generalized resistance resources for better understanding of how people cope successfully to reinforce health" (Olson and Stewart, 1991, p. 7). He also formulated the concept of

FIGURE 2.1. A Theory of Marital Quality and Marital Stability

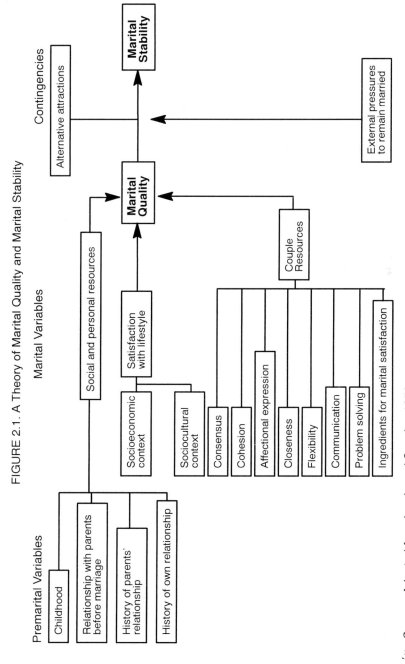

Source: Adapted from Lewis and Spanier, 1979.

"sense of coherence" (SOC) (Antonovsky, 1992), which consists of three dimensions: meaningfulness, comprehensibility, and manageability. Sense of coherence has been defined as a global orientation that expresses the extent to which one has a pervasive and enduring, yet dynamic feeling of confidence that:

1. the stimuli deriving from one's internal and external environments in the course of living are structured, predictable, and explicable;
2. resources are available to meet the demands posed by these stimuli; and
3. the demands are challenges worthy of investment and engagement.

One of the elements that the MASH Model has incorporated is the Circumplex Model (Olson and Stewart, 1991) (see Figure 2.2).

The Circumplex Model has two curvilinear dimensions, *couple cohesion* and *couple adaptability*. It is hypothesized that in clinical populations, the family systems which are balanced in the cohesion/adaptability dimension and score high in the communication dimension will cope better with stress and strain factors than families appearing at either end of the cohesion/adaptability scale and who, at the same time, show a low communication score. Olson refers to the four extreme types as follows:

Name	*Characteristics*
chaotically disengaged	low cohesion—high adaptability
rigidly disengaged	low cohesion—low adaptability
chaotically enmeshed	high cohesion—high adaptability
rigidly enmeshed	high cohesion—low adaptability

However, Olson postulates linearity for the two dimensions of cohesion and adaptability in nonclinical populations. The sample group in his study, as in the present one, was drawn from a nonclinical population. Thus, an underlying premise of this research was that "family systems that are high in cohesion and also in adaptability will function more adequately and reach higher levels of well-being than families scoring low in these dimensions" (Olson and

FIGURE 2.2. Circumplex Model: Sixteen Types of Marital and Family Systems

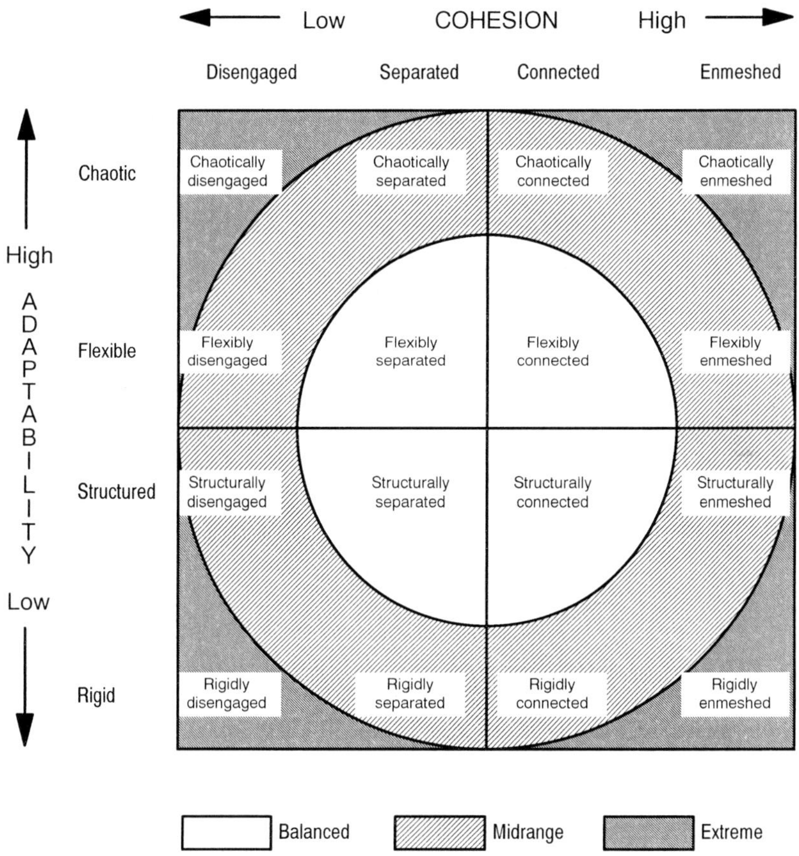

Source: Olson and Stewart, 1990.

Stewart, 1991, p. 4). Using parts of the MASH Model, the study focused on the couple dyad, but also included a number of questions on the individual level that were assumed to be relevant in this context.

The investigation explored the level of marital quality according to the resource variables of the Health and Stress Profile, which are closeness, adaptability, problem-solving ability, and communication skills, as well as consensus, affectional expression, and cohesion of the Dyadic Adjustment Scale. The intent was to broaden this information by identifying ingredients of marital satisfaction from the participants' point of view. Thus, couples conveyed which qualities *they* considered relevant. Fulfilled ingredients function as resources, whereas ingredients that are "desirable" but missing in the relationship indicate deficiencies and reduce the level of marital quality. Low scores on the employed scales (HSP and DAS) also indicate poor quality. Earlier studies investigating marital quality, including our pilot study (Kaslow and Hammerschmidt, 1992), showed the importance of these ingredients as resources. This information was integrated into our model for the subsequent research to compare the importance of these ingredients for long-term, successful marriages drawn from couples in a number of different countries.

For the most part, divorce is the consequence of dissatisfaction in a relationship. The purpose of this research was to investigate how couples are able "to go together through thick and thin" (Kelley, 1983, p. 287) and how they are able to succeed in coping with unavoidable crisis situations. Crises do not always terminate in negative consequences; they can also be accepted as challenges for growth and change. This is congruent with systems theory, which suggests that living systems tend to evolve toward greater complexity. McCubbin and Patterson (1983) propose that "a continuum from bonadaption to maladaption might be a more useful concept to describe the postcrisis adjustment of individuals and couples" (Olson and Stewart, 1991, p. 6). The coping resources are considered as mediating variables between stress and adaptation. Consequently, the question was raised as to which variables distinguish couples with good postcrisis adjustment from those who remain together but in unhappy marriages. Therefore, a retrospective view of the motives for staying together during the difficult stages of marriage was employed.

Marital satisfaction is considered to be a function of resources available, though it cannot be seen exclusively as a result of the present couple interaction. Couple satisfaction represents the level at which the mutual expectations of the partners were fulfilled during the years leading up to the current moment. It is evident that couple satisfaction also affects the resources and vice versa, meaning that satisfaction is included in the feedback loop of resource variables. This raises the probability of escalation. Values, beliefs, and expectations are central determinants for the development of relationships. Shared experiences during many years of a relationship, as well as mastered challenges, will function as resources when they impact on the coping processes of individuals or couples in either a direct or indirect way.

SUMMARY

The present investigation began with the selection of seemingly relevant determinants for successful marriages derived from a pilot study in the United States. The next task was to show how these variables are integrated into the theory of marital quality and marital stability of Lewis and Spanier (1979) and then to reveal the hierarchy of importance of the resources for marital satisfaction. The final target of the research was to extrapolate those variables which may serve as a portrait to guide therapeutic interventions with distressed couples in the direction of achieving greater marital satisfaction.

Chapter 3

Methodology

SAMPLING PROCEDURE

Data were collected in the following countries: Canada, Chile, Germany, Israel, the Netherlands, South Africa, Sweden, and the United States. The general methodology used was the same for all eight countries. The majority of participating couples were recruited by the network sampling approach, which is frequently used when data have to be collected from nonclinical (i.e., not currently in treatment) subjects. This technique is a documented method for collecting data when nonexistent or unattainable lists of population groups create virtually insurmountable barriers to implementing a randomized sampling technique (Kuzel, 1992). The criterion for participation was length of marriage between twenty and forty-six years. The total number of participants was 610 couples.

INSTRUMENTS UTILIZED

This section tracks the shift from the theoretical approach to the empirical investigation, with an explanation of the fundamental concepts of the instruments used.

Dyadic Adjustment Scale

The Dyadic Adjustment Scale (DAS) (Spanier, 1976) has become the most widely used instrument in the family field. It was designed for an overall assessment of dyadic adjustment as well as for measuring its four dimensions separately. The four dimensions are:

1. *Dyadic consensus:* the degree to which the couple agrees on matters of importance to the relationship
2. *Dyadic satisfaction:* the degree to which the partners are satisfied with the present state of the relationship and are committed to its continuance
3. *Dyadic cohesion:* the degree to which the couple engages in activities together
4. *Affection expression:* the extent of agreement regarding demonstration of affection and sexual relations

The concept of dyadic adjustment or dyadic quality is defined as a comprehensive, subjective rating of the couple relationship. The basic structure of the DAS and its subscales was supported in a follow-up study by Spanier and Thompson (1982). They reported that the four factors were robust and had distinct meaning, citing research in which the subscales were used separately. However, they also stated that the subscale affection expression was problematic since two of the four items had small loadings.

The reliability of the DAS as a unidimensional or multidimensional instrument is still under debate. The results of some studies with samples of "distressed" and "nondistressed" couples (Sharpley and Cross, 1982; Crane, Busby, and Larson, 1991) have claimed that the affection expression subscale and the dyadic satisfaction subscale both were problematical. On the other hand, researchers utilizing nonclinical samples (Sabatelli, 1988; Thompson and Spanier, 1983) have reconfirmed rather good psychometric properties for the satisfaction subscale. The reported problem comparing currently distressed and nondistressed couples is to determine the cutoff point for marital distress. Given the continuum of possible scores, it is desirable to recommend a fixed cutoff point. However, labeling couples distressed or nondistressed has to be done carefully, taking into consideration the interdyadic as well as intradyadic differences between couples of subsamples with regard to age, length of marriage, and culture.

Our suggestion is to define three groups, focusing on:

DAS total score: well adapted — nondistressed — distressed
dyadic satisfaction: very satisfied — midrange — dissatisfied

This solution better reflects reality and enables a differentiated analysis. Furthermore, our results show that it is important to analyze both the unidimensional and multidimensional aspects.

The concept of satisfaction is rather subjective, with the degree of satisfaction depending on the fulfillment of expectations. This criterion is essential to the notion of satisfaction as an outcome variable, since these interindividual differences must be taken into account, especially in a cross-cultural context. Considering our multicultural, multinational investigation, we were concerned with the patterns of relationships among the dimensions of marital quality, and how each dimension might be connected to other constructs.

There are a variety of possibilities for measuring couple satisfaction. Subjectivity is best reflected by the single item: "Please circle the point which best describes the degree of happiness, all things considered, of your relationship" (DAS, item 31). This single question is often used, especially in large surveys, because of its functional economy. Although the degrees of happiness and satisfaction are highly correlated, they do not have quite the same meaning. Another question is, how reliable and stable are the elicited self-report statements? The development of satisfaction scales is contingent upon finding the best indicators for satisfaction, based on behavior patterns and thoughts found to be typical for satisfied spouses.

The concept of marital quality or marital adjustment is more global. Satisfaction is one important dimension in addition to consensus and cohesion. Consequently, dyadic adjustment does not strictly represent the degree of dyadic satisfaction, although adjustment and satisfaction have high degrees of shared variance. For example, when measuring satisfaction, gender differences are compensated in DAS total score through the three other subscales. This means that in a unidimensional assessment important information disappears, depending on the expectations of satisfaction with the same degree of measured consensus and cohesion. Furthermore, even the best scale measuring dyadic quality cannot include every potential influence affecting satisfaction.

Health and Stress Profile

The Health and Stress Profile (HSP) (Olson and Stewart, 1991) is a battery of questionnaires developed for the assessment of stress, coping behavior, and resources, as well as adaptation at four levels: individual, couple, family, and work. It is based on the Multisystem Assessment of Stress and Health, the MASH Model. The coping resources are considered as mediating variables between stress and adaptation.

We employed four scales of the HSP for the assessment of coping resources at the couple level. These four resource variables are:

1. *Couple cohesion (closeness)*, defined as the emotional bonding of spouses to each other (Spanier's definition of cohesion is narrower; r = .65)
2. *Couple flexibility*, defined as the ability of the spouses to change their power structure, role relationships, and relationship rules in response to both situational and developmental stress
3. *Couple communication*, referring to empathy, reflective listening, or supportive comments that enable couples to share their changing needs and preferences with each other
4. *Couple problem solving*, meaning defining issues and taking positive steps toward setting goals, in order to arrive at viable solutions to problems and to remain empathic with each other

Problem Rating List

The Problem Rating List contains twenty-one items constructed to investigate potential problem areas within the couple relationship. This questionnaire was employed to assess the degree of issues of conflict between the spouses. Thirteen items are identical with the dyadic consensus subscale (DAS), and eight items were added to cover the whole spectrum of marital life.

Rating List Motives: "Why Did and Do You Stay Together?"

Marital success means stability as well as satisfaction; these are basically independent dimensions. Lewis and Spanier (1979) categorized marriages into four types resulting from the combination of high and low quality with high and low stability. The focus of this long-term marriage (LTM) project is on stable relationships. The rating list was especially designed for this study to investigate the reasons for marital stability in both satisfied and dissatisfied couples and during different stages of marriage (Kaslow and Hammerschmidt, 1992; Hammerschmidt and Kaslow, 1995). The forty-five presented motives were categorized as follows.

Intrinsic motivation. This includes partner-related as well as partnership-related motives:

- Partner-related motives are exclusively related to the partner as a person per se and meet the spouse's healthy needs. For example: "I still find my partner attractive." "I believe I could not find a better partner in spite of a number of difficulties."
- Partnership-related motives are those which express the continuing process of give and take, as well as connectedness. For example: "Our shared experiences have drawn us closely together." "We complement each other in spite of occasional tensions." (See Appendix B, Q.4. for list of motives.)

Values and beliefs. Beliefs function as resources when they serve the coping process in either a direct or an indirect way. Motives listed on the questionnaire include: "I feel responsible to my partner." "Because of religious conviction."

Social norms and expectations, as well as outside pressure. Examples of social norms and expectations include "because of expectations of our family of origin" and "because separation and divorce are considered as social stigma."

Positive problem solving. This refers to both attitude and ability to solve problems. For example: "One cannot give up easily in such crucial matters." "I can contribute something to shaping our marital life."

Extrinsic motivation. This is the consideration of advantages and disadvantages that the relationship offers in economic, practical, or social arenas. For example: "I do not want to accept economic disadvantages." "I enjoy our lifestyle and do not wish to change it."

Neurotic motives. Neurotic motives such as dependency, lack of self-esteem, and in extreme cases, severe pathology. For example: "I am afraid of change." "I have learned to live with a less than satisfactory marriage."

Rating List of "Ingredients for Marital Satisfaction"

Whereas the hypothesized resource variables were explored by four scales of Olson's Health and Stress Profile, the rating list of ingredients for marital satisfaction was employed to prove and broaden the concept of resources. In the pilot study (Kaslow and Hammerschmidt, 1992), the essential ingredients of longevity and satisfaction in marital relationships were investigated by an open-ended questionnaire. The respondents' ideas as to what made their marriages work well provided the basic pool of items that later made up the fixed-choice checklist for this study (see Appendix B, Questionnaire):

Sense of Coherence

Antonovsky (1992) developed formulations about a "sense of coherence" (SOC) and also created an instrument with the same name for measuring this concept. The SOC concept consists of three dimensions: *meaningfulness, comprehensibility,* and *manageability.* SOC has been defined as a global orientation that expresses the extent to which one has a pervasive and enduring, yet dynamic feeling of confidence that:

1. the stimuli deriving from one's internal and external environments in the course of living are structured, predictable, and explicable;
2. resources are available to one to meet the demands posed by these stimuli; and
3. these demands are challenges worthy of investment and engagement.

This self-rating instrument was developed to enable researchers and clinicians to measure individual coping styles, and ultimately to increase the capacity for stress-resilience, thereby making it a health-promoting factor (Antonovsky, 1988).

INSTRUMENTS EMPLOYED: OVERVIEW

The battery of five questionnaires (Q.1.-Q.5.) was organized and standardized by Sharlin and Hammerschmidt for use in participating countries. This battery of self-rating instruments was composed of the following questionnaires and rating scales:

Q.1. General Information Form

1. Personal data: six items
   Self-rated physical health and well-being: one item
   Self-rated degree of happiness during childhood: one item
2. Relationship with parents before marriage: four items
3. History of parents' relationship: three items
4. History of own marital relationship: nine items

This questionnaire was especially designed for this study (Kaslow and Hammerschmidt, 1992).

Q.2. Dyadic Adjustment Scale

1. Dyadic consensus: thirteen items (e.g., regarding family finances, career decisions, matters of recreation)
2. Dyadic satisfaction: ten items (e.g., "In general, how often do you think things between you and your spouse are going well?")
3. Dyadic cohesion: five items (e.g., "How often do you calmly discuss something?")
4. Affectional expression: four items (e.g., extent of agreement regarding demonstration of affection)

The total score represents dyadic adjustment and ranges from 0-151. Of the thirty-two items, thirty are Likert-type (0-5), and two are yes or no. High scores mean a high degree of adjustment. The Israeli study also includes in the DAS two items of the Marital Adjustment Test (Locke and Wallace, 1959).

5. Problem rating list: contains twenty-one items investigating potential problem areas in the couple relationship

Thirteen items are identical with the dyadic consensus subscale, and eight items were added to cover the whole spectrum of marital life (e.g., extent of agreement regarding children, personal freedom, and space). All items are Likert-type. High scores indicate full consensus/no conflict.

Q.3. Health and Stress Profile

1. Couple problem solving: ten items (e.g., "There is little cooperation between us.")
2. Couple communication: ten items (e.g., "My partner is a good listener.")
3. Couple relationship:

   • Subscale, couple cohesion: items 1-19 / odd (e.g., "We ask each other for help.")
   • Subscale, couple flexibility: items 2-20 / even (e.g., "We are flexible in our lifestyle.")

The scores on each scale range from 10 to 50 and are all Likert-type. High scores have a positive meaning.

Q.4. Motives: "Why Did and Do You Stay Together?"

The following rating list was especially designed for this study by Kaslow and Hammerschmidt (1992). Each of the spouses was asked to select three reasons out of forty-five in each of two categories:

1. "Which are the most important to you now?"; and
2. "Which were crucial during the most difficult state of your marriage?" For example: "We complement each other in spite of occasional tension"; "I am convinced that we can resolve our problems"; "I can adjust myself to my partner"; "We have children"; "My financial dependence."

Q.5. Ingredients for Marital Satisfaction

This rating list was also designed especially for the study by Kaslow and Hammerschmidt (1992). Forty-two ingredients were listed, including: mutual trust, mutual support, love, loyalty and

fidelity, shared values, permitting each other individual development, and frequent exchange of ideas. Participants were requested
to indicate a total of ten items under both categories:

Q.5 A: Which ingredients exist presently in their marriage; and
Q.5 B: Which ingredients they would desire.

One more instrument was used in some countries (Sweden, Canada, and Chile). The instrument, called sense of coherence (SOC),
was developed by Antonovsky (1988, 1992).

The SOC consists of twenty-nine items with seven alternatives
on each item, all of which are Likert-type. The total score varies
between 29 and 203.

VALIDITY AND RELIABILITY ASPECTS

In the United States and Canada, the original forms of the DAS
(Spanier, 1976) and the HSP scales (Olson and Stewart, 1991) were
used. Translations, tested with regard to psychometric qualities, that
were utilized in Germany were the DAS (Hahlweg, Hank, and
Klam, 1990) and HSP (Schneewind, Weiss, and Olson, 1992). The
researchers in Chile, Israel, South Africa, Sweden, and the Netherlands had to develop their own versions. The original English version of all employed instruments was translated into Spanish, He-
brew, Afrikaans, Swedish, and Dutch in each respective country,
then back to English and again into the native languages. For the
German study, only the questionnaires 1, "General Information,"
4, "Motives," and 5, "Ingredients" had to be translated. Each step of
this translation procedure had to be done by different persons to
discover divergences. Although the translations may have changed
the nuances of some questions, the data collection instruments were
sufficiently similar to tap into data that are comparable across the
eight country samples.

The two rating lists, Q.4 "Motives" and Q.5 "Ingredients," were
designed as checklists but not as questionnaires because they do not
fulfill the appropriate psychometric criteria. The data gathered and
analyzed according to the two rating lists have only the quality of

ordinal scales with the corresponding implications for statistical evaluation.

PROCEDURE:
HOW THE STUDY WAS CONDUCTED

Each couple received two sets of forms, one for the husband and one for the wife. They were instructed to respond completely on their own, not to compare answers with the spouse, and only to compare and discuss reactions after completion. They were requested to enclose the forms in the stamped envelopes provided and to mail immediately upon completion. Since neither name, profession, nor address were asked, anonymity could be guaranteed. The following describes the procedure used in each of the eight countries:

1. The fifty-six respondents in Chile came from the metropolitan region of Santiago. Questionnaires were mailed to them after verbal inquiries.

2. In Israel, forms were sent out to 120 couples, all of whom were Jewish and Caucasian. Of these, eighty-seven couples returned usable questionnaires. In this sample, 55 percent of men and 60 percent of women were Israeli-born. The second largest group was born in Eastern Europe—36.7 percent of the men and 26.7 percent of the women. The remainder were from Western Europe and the former Soviet Union. Fifteen percent of the Israeli sample were Holocaust survivors, all of whom had come from Eastern Europe.

3. Of the 126 couples to whom questionnaires were sent in Sweden, ninety-five couples responded. Of these, five did not fill in the SOC.

4. In Germany, 250 questionnaires were distributed through ministers, physicians, colleagues, and friends. The 105 respondents were from all regions of the former West Germany. All participants were offered a summary of the results of the study, if they provided their address for this purpose.

5. In the United States, of the 100 couples to whom questionnaires were sent in part two of the study, sixty replied by the due date, but five of them were unusable. After the original deadline passed, follow-up postcards were mailed to nonrespondents, netting two additional returns, for a total of fifty-seven usable couple re-

sponses. The respondent couples, identified only as Caucasian, re-
sided in nine states across the United States, reflecting a regional
diversity. Although in the pilot study almost all of the couples were
Jewish, in the second portion the vast majority were Protestant.

6. In South Africa, the questionnaires were distributed through
the directors of seventeen societies working under the umbrella of
the National Council for Family and Marriage in South Africa
(FAMSA). All were advised that a nonclinical population was to be
approached. A total of ninety-one completed sets of questionnaires
were returned, with fifty-one from the Johannesburg area and forty
from those distributed by ten societies in other areas, such as Cape
Town, Durban, Benoni, Kempton Park, Mossel Bay, Pietermaritzburg, and Welkom, providing a diverse picture. Most respondents
were English-speaking, white, middle-class couples. Only one Asian
and one African couple participated.

7. In the Netherlands, of the sixty-eight nonclinical couples who
were approached by the researcher, fifty-four agreed to cooperate.
Four of them had been married less than twenty-five years and were
thus not included in the study.

8. In Canada, questionnaires were sent by mail to 110 couples;
the final sample included sixty-seven of these.

LIMITATIONS OF THE STUDY

The results must be interpreted cautiously since true representa-
tiveness can only be obtained from larger randomized samples. A
special selection process results from the participation of volun-
teers. Only willing and responsive persons are reached. In addition,
people refuse to participate for various reasons; for example, they
lack time or they have doubts about the purpose of the investigation. Avoidance may be a factor if they dislike the topic of the study,
though we do not know how many nonreturns occurred for this
reason.

Given that educational systems are different in the eight countries, information regarding educational level of participants is difficult to compare. Likewise, data about income allows only general
statements regarding socioeconomic status and standard of living.
Nonetheless, the data from all eight country samples show that the

majority of participants were drawn from the middle and upper-middle classes. In spite of the aforementioned limitations, these findings can be considered typical of LTM couples; the similarities found among respondents in all eight countries appear to be significant and to indicate fundamental ingredients that contribute to LTM. The interpretation of results in regard to differences still needs to be done cautiously. Divergences could be as much typical for the culture as for the specific but hidden characteristics of the sample.

ANALYSIS OF DATA: STATISTICAL TOOLS

To create a sample description of each country, the following tools were used: frequencies, percent distributions, ranges, means, and standard deviations. The samples were then grouped according to gender, age, length of marriage, and employment (working full-time, working part-time, or retired). Couple satisfaction as the criterion variable is divided into three levels:

1. Very satisfied: Both spouses score half a standard deviation (SD) over the mean or more
2. Midrange: Between half a standard deviation over and under the mean
3. Dissatisfied: One or both spouses score more than half a standard deviation under the mean

The hypotheses for the study were as follows:

1. Couples who are very satisfied share many common characteristics across cultures, religious groups, and socioeconomic strata.
2. The mean of couple satisfaction for women is lower than for men.
3. Couple satisfaction is positively associated with cohesion, adaptability, dyadic consensus, good communication, and problem-solving skills.
4. If both partners are very satisfied, the marriage is based on intrinsic motivation. If one or both spouses are dissatisfied,

the marriage is based on normative, extrinsic, or even "neurotic" motives.

5. Women and men have different priorities with reference to what constitutes a fulfilling partnership.
6. Marital satisfaction is positively associated with well-being and physical health.
7. The mean of marital satisfaction is higher after retirement.
8. Couple satisfaction is positively associated with the degree of happiness during childhood.
9. A connection exists between SOC and marital satisfaction.
10. There are gender differences on SOC.

The significance of group differences was estimated using three different measures: t-test, analysis of variance (ANOVA) and d-statistics. Pearson's coefficient of correlation was used for determining the interdependence of variables. Finally, the best predictors for marital satisfaction were identified by regression analysis (stepwise).

Comparison of the Eight Countries

Data from the United States, Canada, Germany, Sweden, the Netherlands, Israel, South Africa, and Chile were analyzed. Researchers in each country interpreted their own data. Afterward, all raw data were forwarded to the Center for Research and Study of the Family (CRSF) in Israel for cross-cultural analysis and comparison. For data comparison analysis among the eight countries, the following statistical tools were used: t-test and one-way analysis of variance; multiple regression analysis, stepwise; and acyclic connected graph (Pearson's correlation). (See Chapter 7 for comparative analysis among countries.)

PART II:
FINDINGS

Chapter 4

Reports of the United States and Canada

This chapter is the first of three summarizing the reports of the participating countries. It presents the data from the United States and Canada, the two countries in North America. Chapter 5 will summarize the findings from Germany, Sweden, and the Netherlands, the three Western European countries involved. Chapter 6 presents the results of the studies in Israel, South Africa, and Chile; each of these countries is unique, and they are located in three different continents, so the data contained therein are drawn from quite diverse population groups. In Chapter 7, the findings from the eight participating countries are compared on the same measures and scales. The findings have been interpreted differently in each country, from individual cultural perspectives, emphasizing different issues that may not have been studied by the others. Although a specific outline was given to each of the researchers, not all were able to follow it exactly, which may pose some limitations on the comparability of the data.

THE UNITED STATES

The Pilot Study

Prior to launching this multinational research project, a pilot study was conducted in the United States with a small group of twenty couples. The couples were divided into three categories—satisfied, midrange, and not satisfied. The cutoff points were established using

Material on the United States is taken from Kaslow and Hammerschmidt (1992). Long-term "good" marriages: The seemingly essential ingredients. *Journal of Couples Therapy,* 3(2/3), 15-38. Reprint permission granted by The Haworth Press, 1999.

Spanier's (1976) scoring system on the Dyadic Adjustment Scale (DAS). The mean satisfaction score in Spanier's study population of over 700 couples was 40.5. Thus, the ten couples who scored between 41 and 48 were placed in the satisfied group. Their total scores on the DAS fell between 120 and 136. Thus, both members of these couples had a mean score that was well above the total DAS for Spanier's study group, which was 114.8. The mid-range couples scored between 37 and 40 on the satisfaction scale and 109 to 119 on the total DAS, respectively. The unsatisfied couples scored between 32 and 36 on the satisfaction scale and 101 to 108 on their total DAS, with only one exception, as noted later.

One factor worthy of mention in this regard was the amount of variance between the partners' responses. In the satisfied group, there was great consistency in the level of satisfaction and the overall score. Among the midrange couples, more differences appeared.

In comparing the three groups of ten satisfied, four midrange, and six dissatisfied couples, we found some actual although not statistically significant differences in the variables attributed to the longevity of marriage. Love, mutual respect and trust, shared interests and value system, shared love for children, the ability to give and take, and flexibility were all mentioned much more frequently by satisfied couples, less so by midrange pairs, and least by dissatisfied couples. Sensitivity to the needs of one's spouse appears only in the group of satisfied couples (30 percent). An equalitarian relationship with many complementary features was also cited as important by satisfied couples, but less frequently than the factors cited earlier.

Interestingly, having a shared interest in their children was cited by all as important in their lives together, but *only* by dissatisfied couples as a reason for the longevity of their marriages (33 percent of this group). The satisfied group stayed together because they wanted to be with each other, and not for the sake of the children. The dissatisfied group also disclosed that they experienced a lack of affectional expressiveness and support from each other. The midrange couples revealed a deficit in the arena of "good communication."

Fun, humor, and playfulness rarely appear as factors in the responses of the midrange and dissatisfied couples; i.e., these do not seem to be a vital part of their lives together. This is in contrast to the fact that 40 percent of the satisfied couples stated that they have fun together and treasure it. A *strong sense of self* is cited only in the midrange group as an important contributory factor to the longevity of their marriages (38 percent).

For two variables, *good sexual relationship* (30 percent in all groups) and the *availability of privacy and personal space* when desired (15 percent), few differences emerged among the three groups. *Good joint problem-solving ability* turned out to be the item ranked as the key and major factor contributing to satisfaction for all three groups. It was mentioned by 70 percent of both the satisfied and the midrange couples, and by 33 percent of the dissatisfied pairs.

In response to the question "To what factors do you attribute the longevity of your marriage?" the satisfied couples provided the greatest number of responses:

- Satisfied—7.25 answers per person (mean)
- Midrange—5.12 answers per person (mean)
- Dissatisfied—3.75 answers per person (mean)

These results can be interpreted as a reflection of their greater awareness of what is conducive to their happiness and an appreciation of the emotional richness of their lives. Conversely, the paucity of responses of the dissatisfied couples adequately represents their constricted relationships and overall discontent.

Many of the findings reported above are consistent with observations, study findings, and conclusions presented by other authors. Almost four decades ago, Burgess and Wallin (1953) found that the presence of *good joint problem-solving ability* bore a high positive correlation with relationship satisfaction. Nawran (1967) observed that good communication and sensitivity to the feelings of the partner characterize a happy marriage. Beavers' (1985) work highlighted the fact that successful marriages are usually *equalitarian* in power distribution. He found that a *shared value system* is also an important factor. Schwarzenhauer (1980) found *shared interests* to be a major element in happy marriages.

In Miller and Olson's (1976) delineation of the Circumplex Model, they presented two axes of coordinates: closeness and control. The existence of both involvement←→isolation, and rigidity←→chaos characterize dysfunctional relationships. In long-term satisfying relationships, one sees *adaptability* rather than rigidity, *order* rather than chaos, and a *sense of attachment and belonging* rather than isolation or alienation.

In contrast to what Willi (1975/1990) found in his work on couples in collusion, alluded to earlier, in this study it appears that those who ranked as highly satisfied in their marriages had resolved whatever trauma they experienced, either prior to marriage or early in their time together, and had been able to cope with crises and transitions in their adult years. Thus, they are present and future oriented, rather than having their energy bound up in the past and allowing their history to exert a negative influence on the here and now. In addition, both seem to engage in progressive rather than regressive behaviors—apparently a hallmark of the healthy, satisfied couple.

Influence of Parents' Marriage

Schwarzenhauer (1980) ascertained that the best chance for a harmonious marriage exists when both spouses have parents who had a good marital relationship. When individuals come from families marred by much marital discord and turbulence, or by bitter divorces, the prognosis is less than favorable. This phenomenon can be interpreted in different ways. One is, as mentioned previously, that in dysfunctional families the likelihood that children will develop personality disorders or other pathological syndromes is much higher. Emotional stability emanating from a consistently loving environment is the best precondition for and precursor of the ability to make a commitment to a long-term, intimate relationship. Another explanation is that good social competence and interpersonal skills, including the willingness and capacity to be sensitive to and concerned about others, is learned in childhood. Being able to value the I, Thou, and We (Buber, 1937) in a relationship and give them appropriate weightings in different situations is a philosophy and skill best learned from contented parents who not only nurture, guide, and set limits but serve as exemplary role models.

No specific data on the relationship between the satisfaction levels of the couples who participated and that of their parents was obtained. None of the questions were phrased specifically enough to tap into this data. This is difficult to do given that the assessment of one's parents' marriage is subjective, retrospective, and has strong emotional overtones, rendering the reliability of the responses somewhat dubious. Also, the perceptions of what constitutes happiness may change over time. Indeed, the entire question of the impact and influence of the parents' marriage on their offspring is a very complex one.

Hopefully, this multinational study, including the pilot phase, will generate interest among other researchers to further pursue the study of the key variables in the intergenerational transmission process (Bowen, 1988). Fortunately, no one is inescapably affected by their parents. Thus, those coming from unhappy, dysfunctional, "pathological" families of origin can, through life experience, through seeking other role models, and/or through therapy, learn more effective ways of coping, master the unfinished issues and tasks of childhood, find healthy channels for satisfying their deficit (D) and being (B) needs (Maslow, 1970), and become able to trust sufficiently to make a commitment to an exclusive love relationship.

It was hypothesized in this study that some dissatisfied couples who stay together do so in an act of loyalty to their parents, who they know disapprove of divorce and/or would be profoundly distressed if they were to divorce. Unfortunately, inherent in this type of loyalty is a degree of martyrdom that can lead to enormous unhappiness and which may ultimately be converted into any number of physical or emotional maladies.

"Words of Wisdom" Regarding Marital Satisfaction

Study respondents were asked what advice they would give to others to help them achieve satisfying relationships. Since advice can be derived as much from positive as from negative experiences, we lumped together the responses from the three categories of subjects. In descending order of frequency, the responses were:

1. Give and take, compromise   38%
2. Establish and maintain good communication   35%
3. Respect your spouse and treat him or her as an equal   28%
4. Establish a tight (close, cohesive) family   25%

5. Be supportive of your spouse	23%
6. Be sensitive to and considerate of the needs of your spouse	23%
7. Trust each other, be honest	23%
8. Maintain a balance between individuality and couplehood	23%
9. Love each other and be committed to the relationship	23%
10. Have fun together as often as possible	18%
11. Marry someone with similar values, or develop these together	8%
12. Share interests and activities so time together is well spent	18%
13. Choose a partner with a similar background.	10%
14. Choose the "right" partner	8%
15. Work together for financial security	8%
16. Be affectionate, stay in touch sensually	8%
17. Solve problems as they arise	8%
18. Be friends	8%

Fennell (1987) conducted a study of 147 couples, all in first marriages that had lasted over twenty years. He did not seem to limit the upper range of number of years married nor did he report ages and other demographic characteristics of respondents, so the two studies cannot be compared on these variables. He and his assistants located subjects through a "search and referral method" (p. 8) that seems analogous to our networking procedure. He also utilized Spanier's Dyadic Adjustment Scale (1976) as the main instrument for rating subjects on marital satisfaction and created a survey instrument through which couples were asked "what they believed were the characteristics they and their spouses possessed that resulted in their long-term marriages" (Fennell, 1987, p. 4). Nonetheless, his study and ours were somewhat similar in methodology, in instructions to respondents, and in objectives.

In his study, Fennell found that the following eight characteristics reappeared with the greatest frequency:

1. Lifetime commitment to marriage
2. Loyalty to spouse and the expectation of reciprocity
3. Strong, shared moral values

4. Respect for spouse as best friend, and self-disclosure to each other
5. Commitment to sexual fidelity
6. Desire to be a good parent
7. Faith in God and spiritual commitment
8. Good companion to spouse—spend a great deal of enjoyable time together over the course of lifetime

His major finding was that husbands and wives in satisfactory marriages of twenty-plus years' duration express high congruence regarding what they think are the important characteristics contributing to their long-term unions. Similarly, Murstein (1980) found that in successful marriages, the partners possess value consensus and role congruence. Our findings also pointed to a high level of concordance in each couple's assessment of the qualities and variables that make their marriages work well for them.

A comparison of the characteristics Fennell's respondents highlighted and those reported by the researchers and clinicians at a conference on healthy families ("Healthy Families," 1990) show much overlap with some variation. Fennell's work emphasizes the best friend, fidelity, and commitment factors more; the conference participants placed much greater weight on the importance of good problem solving and coping skills. Both found that the variable of a spiritual orientation or transcendental value system seemed central; this does not emerge as quite as significant from our study population, although it was cited by some of the couples.

Our respondents, given the freedom to create their own list of essential ingredients, included all of the other variables that appear on both lists, plus several more. Additional attributes most emphasized include:

1. Being patient and understanding
2. Listening well
3. Doing exciting activities together, including travel, and avoiding repetition and boredom
4. Continued sexual attraction and mutual sexual enjoyment
5. A great deal of expressed affection
6. Loyalty and fidelity to one another

7. Noninterference by both sets of parents, yet closeness to children and extended family
8. Helping each other when requested to do so
9. Being supportive of each other's wishes, careers, and dreams
10. Seeing the spouse as a good parent
11. Both are trustworthy, and respect each other's integrity
12. Like each other as individuals

Summary of the Pilot Study

Healthy individuals with a high well-being are most apt to be attracted to a partner who is also self-actualizing and has a good self-image, yet is able to be considerate of, sensitive to, and capable of commitment to a significant other. Such pairings seem to produce the kind of long-term marital satisfaction that is being studied here.

The words of wisdom elicited from the study respondents subsume and go beyond the characteristics most often cited as prototypical of healthy couples and families. The essential ingredients for long-term satisfying marriages most frequently given by our study respondents were the following:

1. Good problem-solving and coping skills
2. Trust in each other that includes fidelity, integrity, and feeling "safe"
3. Permanent commitment to the marriage
4. Open, honest, good communication
5. Enjoy spending time together, have fun together, good sense of humor—yet appreciate some spaces in togetherness for separate activities
6. Shared value system, interests, and activities
7. Consideration, mutual appreciation, and reciprocity—easy give and take
8. Deep and abiding love for each other, enriched by being dear friends and lovers; continue to find each other attractive, appealing, desirable, and interesting

The cohesive family unit stressed in the literature to date does typify the satisfied couples in this sample. They have a sense of belonging to their respective families of origin, remain appropriately attached to their adult children and grandchildren, and are characterized by loyalty rather than indifference to significant others. It appears that these couples have intuitively and deliberately fashioned for themselves a dynamic and flexible "recipe" for a satisfying, long-term marriage. Similarity and congruence of background regarding religion, education, and lifestyle emerge as key factors. Endogamy rather than exogamy seems to hold part of the key to the kind of shared values that are conducive to long-term pleasure and satisfaction.

Part 2 of the U.S. Study

Based on the results obtained in the pilot study, it was possible to move ahead with a different and larger sample of fifty-seven couples and to expand the scope of the research to include eight countries. The responses of the fifty-seven couples in Part 2 of the U.S. study closely matched those received from the original group, and the findings are quite similar despite differences in study populations.

Sociodemographic Data

In Part 2 of the U.S. study, the 114 subjects (57 couples) ranged in age from 44 to 74 years, with a mean age of 56.8 years. No significant differences were noted among groups (Kaslow and Robinson, 1996). Men were slightly older than women (57.6 versus 56.1 years). All couples met the criterion of having been married between 25 and 46 years at the time they responded, with an average length of marriage of 35 years. The group of dissatisfied couples had been married slightly longer (36.2 years) than the other two groups (34.9 for the midrange and 34.7 for the satisfied couples). The individuals' ages at the time of marriage varied from 15 to 38; females averaged 20.7 years and males averaged 22.2 years. The satisfied couples reported an average age at marriage of 22.2 years; their mean age at time of marriage was slightly older than that of both the dissatisfied group (20.8) and the midrange group (20.5).

The couples cited various lengths of premarital acquaintance, ranging from one month to ten years. The average length was over three years. No discernible trends in the length of premarital acquaintance were noted among the groups; however, the greatest variability in the length of acquaintance prior to marrying existed in the satisfied couples. Less than 18 percent of the total sample had known each other for less than a year before marrying. Contrary to common expectations, 24 percent of the satisfied couples knew each other for less than a year, while only 13 percent of the mid-range and 8 percent of the dissatisfied couples had such short pre-marital acquaintance. This leads to a hypothesis that something other than length of premarital acquaintance predicts marital lon-gevity and satisfaction.

Three women and two men reported having been married pre-viously; four of these five had children from their first union. No information was collected as to the reason for the dissolution of those first marriages. The remaining 109 individuals (96 percent) stated that their current marriage was their only one.

All but two couples reported having children, with the average number of children per couple from the present marriage being 2.9 (range from 0 to 6 children per couple). Although not statistically significant, the mean number of children of the midrange couples was slightly higher (3.3 children) than that reported by either the dissatis-fied or the satisfied couples (both 2.6 children). Predictable from the fact that they had married at a slightly older age was that the satisfied couples were older when their first child arrived (24.3 years) than were either the dissatisfied (23.7 years) or the midrange couples (22.9). No differences in the number of years the couples were married before the arrival of that first child were noted among groups.

Although a trend was observed toward greater education as the ratings of marital satisfaction increased, the mean for all groups indicated some college education (education: 14.1 years, range 8 to 26 years). This level exceeds the educational level of the average American. This clustering occurred despite a concerted effort on the part of the researchers to locate people with a wide variety of levels of educational attainment. Among those reporting total number of years of education, approximately half had received some kind of schooling beyond high school, and half had completed twelve years of education or less. In the analysis of nonresponders whose approximate educational level was known to the researchers, it appeared that a greater percentage of those with college educations failed to respond than did those with only high school educations. Although above the average of the American public, this result is below that reported by the participants in the pilot study, who were drawn from a highly educated social stratum with 87 percent noting some college education, over 50 percent indicating postbaccalaureate training, and 33 percent reporting doctorates (Kaslow and Hammerschmidt, 1992). That the results of the current study are similar to those obtained in the original study despite these differences in educational levels lends additional credibility to the pilot study.

As in the pilot study, 95 percent of the couples reported having the same religion. However, in contrast to the first study, in which 75 percent of the respondents were Jewish, a deliberate attempt was made to tap a more diverse sample in this study. Consequently, in the second sample only 5 percent of the respondents who answered the religion item were Jewish, 10 percent were Catholic, 80 percent were Protestant, and 4 percent checked "other" (6 percent left this question blank). Many of the respondents were drawn from networks to which the second author had entrée, almost all of which have strong Protestant religious affiliations (Kaslow and Robison, 1996).

In this sample, 54 percent of the individuals reported working full-time, an additional 14 percent worked part-time, and 32 percent reported not working. Thus, a considerably lower percentage of individuals in this sample were gainfully employed than the 92.5 percent of participants in the pilot study. No discernible differences were noted among the three groups, although between the genders, males were more likely to report working full-time (61 percent versus 46 percent), and females were more apt not to work (37 percent versus 28 percent).

In the pilot study, questions were asked about income levels. These questions were deleted when the study was expanded due to a lack of comparability across countries. Replacing these questions was a more general item that asked participants to rate their own economic status. Excellent was chosen by 9 percent, 22 percent checked "very good," 39 percent reported "good," 29 percent "fairly good," 0 percent "bad," and 1 percent "very bad." We do not know what parameters were utilized in these ratings as none were provided by the researchers. However, it was clear that reports of high economic status (median ratings of "good") were present among both the midrange and satisfied groups and that the least satisfied couples had the lowest economic status (reporting a median rating between "good" and "fairly good").

Most respondents (85 percent) reported "good" or "very good" health, with a greater percentage expressing moderate or poor health among the dissatisfied couples (27 percent, versus 17 percent for the midrange couples and 11 percent for the satisfied couples). It appears that the problems of poor health, chronic illness, and/or restricted life choices spill over and affect the overall rating of marital satisfaction (see Barth, 1993, on chronic illness and the family).

In terms of any correlation between length of parental marriage and marital longevity in this sample, the average length of parental marriage was 41.4 years (range 3 to 68 years). The dissatisfied couples had the greatest number of divorced parents (15 percent, compared to 3 percent of the midrange and 7 percent of the satisfied couples), with the corresponding shortest average length of marriage (37.6 years, compared to 47.9 years for the midrange and 41.1 years for the satisfied couples), and the lowest rating of parental happiness in marriage (54 percent being rated as "very happy" or "fairly happy," compared to 80 percent of the midrange and 73 percent of the satisfied group). These results support Schwarzenhauer's (1980) statement that the best chance for a harmonious marriage exists when both individuals have parents who had a good marital relationship. As in other aspects of family functioning, there appears to be a strong tendency toward an intergenerational transmission process (Bowen, 1988) in both marital satisfaction and divorce (Kaslow and Schwartz, 1987).

Dyadic Satisfaction Subscale

As indicated previously, respondent couples were divided into three groups—satisfied, midrange, and dissatified—based upon cutoff points established on the dyadic satisfaction subscale (DSS) of the DAS (Spanier, 1976). High scores on this scale are purported to indicate a commitment to the continuance of the relationship and satisfaction with it in its present state (Spanier, 1989). The mean satisfaction score reported in Spanier's study population of over

200 couples was 40.5. Therefore, the 29 out of 57 responding couples (just short of 50 percent, as in the pilot study) in which both partners scored above that mark (between 41 and 48) were placed in the satisfied group.

Their total scores on the DAS fell between 106 and 148, with a mean score of 125.1, compared to a mean of 114.8 for Spanier's normative married population. Thus, the group classified as satisfied herein reflects an average dyadic adjustment that is half a standard deviation above the normative group reported by Spanier.

Midrange couples (Beavers, 1982) were defined as those in which the lowest score of either partner was found to be within half a standard deviation below the mean of Spanier's study population (scores between 37 and 40). Fifteen couples fell in this group. Their total scores on the DAS were between 96 and 126, with a mean score of 113.9, just slightly below the average of Spanier's married normative sample. Of the remaining 13 couples, each had at least one member who scored below 37 on the DSS, and thus they have been classified as constituting the dissatisfied group. Their DSS scores ranged from 25 to 47, with total scores on the DAS ranging from 83 to 140 (mean = 105.5). These average DAS scores fell half a standard deviation below those established by Spanier's normative sample. Thus, almost a quarter of the couples scored midrange on marital satisfaction indices, while a fraction less were ranked as dissatisfied (Kaslow and Hammerschmidt, 1992). A similar relative consistency of responses by pairs again appeared in the satisfied group; the largest amount of variation in responses occurred within the dissatisfied group. Given that results in the current study were almost identical with those obtained in the pilot study, they seem to validate the original findings.

Couples' Problem-Solving Ability

In a comparative assessment of the couples' ability to solve problems in stressful situations, the satisfied couples reported less impulsive and more cooperative, supportive, and flexible ways of resolving problems than did the other two groups. They reported being less isolated from each other than those in the other two categories, yet noted an ability to establish appropriate space between themselves to allow for the resolution of the problem and some private time. They were less affected by each others' moods; that is, they have and can maintain their own feelings and mood states.

The midrange group reported better problem-solving skills than the dissatisfied group; however, they appeared to be more rigid and controlling than the satisfied couples and found it difficult to create the space necessary to think through and resolve the problem, separately or jointly. In light of Gottman and Krokoff's (1989) findings concerning the relationship between isolation, marital dissatisfaction, and later divorce, we note that the coping strategy of isolation, as indicated by items such as "we become more isolated and independent" and "we stay out of each other's way," while used by all groups, was used more by the dissatisfied group.

Couples' Communication

Reports on couple communication patterns also showed considerable predictability. The satisfied couples reported more effective communication strategies than those in the midrange group, who utilized better strategies than those in the dissatisfied group. Factors that enhanced communication effectiveness, identified consistently by all groups, included honesty and not expecting the other to engage in "mind reading" to know what is wanted or felt. Closely related to a lack of mind reading is assertiveness in expressing wants and needs. The dissatisfied couples reported less frequent use of assertive communication than did the other two groups. They also reported being more likely to withhold negative comments out of fear of their spouse's anger, a situation which could result in pseudomutual communications (Wynne et al., 1958). They, along with the midrange couples, indicated a more frequent use of put-downs than did the satisfied couples. The satisfied couples reported a stronger perception of their partners as good listeners, while the other groups conveyed a perceived lack of sharing of feelings by their partners. Instead, the dissatisfied group noted their partner's tendency to "stonewall" (Gottman and Krokoff, 1989) or give them the "silent treatment" when dealing with a problem.

Couples' Assessment of Their Relationship

As anticipated, flexibility was greater among the satisfied couples than among the other two groups. This concurs with a key characteristic of healthy couples identified at the 1990 Family Therapy Conference ("Healthy Families," 1990). Satisfied pairs are willing to ask each other for help, to share leadership, to consult when making decisions, and to engage in joint decision making. In the face of difficulties, a tendency toward compromise and creativity in handling differences was noted as marital satisfaction increased. Togetherness is a top priority for the satisfied couples, and a feeling of closeness is reported. They enjoy each other as friends, are easily able to think of things to do in tandem, and have fun doing things together. Yet they express an appreciation for their partners' having separate friends. In the midrange group, more rigidity in their ability to change their ways of handling tasks is reported than in both those who are satisfied and dissatisfied. It is hypothesized that those who are dissatisfied may be less invested in the marital relationship and therefore more indifferent about how things get done. Perhaps they have given up battling but still do not want to divorce.

Motivation to Stay Together

Respondents were asked to choose three potential motives from among a list of forty-four possibilities that would indicate (1) why they stay in their marriage now and (2) why they stayed together during the most difficult stage in their marriage. These directions seemed confusing to many respondents, who frequently checked off ten or more reasons, thereby altering the nature of the inquiry. Nonetheless, the query yielded responses indicating the main reasons why they remain married: belief that marriage is a partnership for life (76 percent); love (57 percent); sense of responsibility toward the partner (38 percent); an enjoyment of their established lifestyle and wish not to change it (32 percent); religious convictions about the sanctity of marriage (31 percent); sense of closeness resulting from shared experiences throughout life (31 percent); appreciation of closeness and comfort with each other (28 percent); and continuing attraction to the partner (25 percent). The satisfied group chose more internally motivated reasons (love and the value of lifelong marital commitment) than the externally imposed motives and standards selected by the dissatisfied group (responsibility to partner and religious commitment).

During the separately designated most difficult time of their married lives, the most crucial reasons for staying together included many of the same reasons listed above, suggesting that the respondents did not lose sight of why they were doing what they were doing. In all groups, commitment to a partnership for life was the primary reason for remaining in the marriage during difficult times (49 percent). However, for the satisfied group, love was endorsed as an important component (47 percent), something that was not mentioned with nearly the frequency in the other two groups (15 percent of the dissatisfied group and 10 percent of the midrange group). Instead, more externally motivating factors, such as responsibility to children (35 percent), religious conviction (26 percent), and the fear of the negative impact of a marital dissolution upon one's career (26 percent), played a more dominant role.

Ingredients for Marital Satisfaction

The final survey instrument was designed to elicit perceptions of: (1) what ingredients conducive to satisfaction exist in the marriage, and (2) what features the respondent would desire to have as a part of the marriage. A list of forty-two possibilities was offered, and respondents were asked to choose (1) up to ten that currently exist in their marriage and (2) the ten ingredients they most desire. This proved to be a formidable task, as indicated by the numerous comments written in explaining that they could not choose just ten. A number of people checked off all forty-two choices, thus supporting Gottman's (1994) contention that assessment of marital satisfaction by the self-report method is largely a global judgment about the marriage as a whole, with the net result that happily married couples endorse almost any positive item.

Among the ingredients marked as essential for marital satisfaction and currently existing in the marriage, those endorsed by over 50 percent of the respondents are: love (82 percent); mutual trust (81 percent); mutual respect (77 percent); mutual support (68 percent); corresponding religious beliefs (65 percent); loyalty and fidelity (59 percent); mutual give and take (56 percent); similar philosophy of life (56 percent); enjoyment of shared fun and humor (52 percent); shared interests (51 percent); and shared interests in their children (50 percent). Among the three groups, no significant differences were found in their perceptions of the most essential ingredients, although more variability was noted in the responses of the dissatisfied group than in those of the other two groups.

In describing qualities that they would desire in a marriage, numerous respondents marked none of the items and/or wrote in comments such as "my marriage is perfect" or "I have everything I want in my marriage." Items desired in marriage identified by the other participants are: financial and economic security (27 percent); mutual sexual fulfillment (22 percent); expression of affection (20 percent); openness, honesty, candor (18 percent); frequent exchange of ideas (18 percent); consensus about sexual behavior (18 percent); good problem-solving ability (18 percent); sensitivity and consideration for the needs of spouse (17 percent); good listening (17 percent); doing interesting things together (17 percent).

Many of the items marked on this list of qualities that the participants desired to have or improve in their marriage were identified elsewhere in the survey as valuable components of a satisfying marriage. However, two new considerations emerged. First, financial concerns, a developmentally appropriate issue for adults who have launched their children from the nest and begun looking forward to their own retirement and its subsequent reduction of income, rose to the fore. Although no differences were noted in the percentage of respondents in each level of marital satisfaction or of each gender who indicated their desire for economic security, when viewed by age, differences do emerge. Only 25 percent of those between forty-four and fifty-four listed financial worries, while 38 percent of those in the next decade (fifty-five to sixty-four years of age) voiced their desire for economic security. Although more than one-eighth of the sample population was sixty-five years of age or older, none of them listed a desire for financial security in their marriage. One possible explanation is that these individuals undertook more planning prior to their retirement. Fifty percent of those who indicated this desire rated their current economic condition as only fairly good or worse, compared to only 23 percent of those who did not indicate a desire for financial security.

The other major issue not previously raised concerned sexual fulfillment. Approximately half of those of each gender marked statements indicating a desire for mutual sexual fulfillment in their relationship and/or consensus about sexual behavior. No differences in age were noted between genders, with the average age of the females being 57.5 years and the average of males being 57.7 years, nearly paralleling the overall group average ages of 56.1 years for females and 57.6 years for males. A trend was noted among the various levels of satisfaction, with 59 percent of the individuals in the satisfied couples marking a desire for change in the sexual area, 43 percent of the midrange individuals, and 38 percent of those who were classified as dissatisfied. It is hypothesized that those couples who are least satisfied are more concerned with other areas of their marital adjustment, while those who are more satisfied and have worked through other issues have this as a residual concern; it may be one in which they have had less discussion and guidance as to potential solutions or have accepted decreased desire and frequency as a consequence of aging.

The results of this study confirm empirically many of the notions held intuitively by clinicians who work with couples in long-term marriages; these results have implications for interventions with couples who present in a state of dissatisfaction and distress. This study distills the major "essential ingredients" associated with higher levels of marital satisfaction. In this, as in other portions of the larger study, the importance of commitment to the continuation and growth of the marital relationship predominates in the self-reports of satisfied couples. Indeed, over three-fourths of respondents listed this quality as essential to their current satisfaction. Because such a vast majority rated commitment so high, it was not possible to substantiate Rollins and Cannon's (1974) report that a decline in personal commitment corresponds with a decline in marital satisfaction. However, a decline in marital satisfaction does not consistently lead to a decline in commitment to the marriage. In the less satisfied couples and in more stressful times, a "social commitment" (Johnson, 1982) and external pressure may come into play through the individual's perceptions of moral pressure, of other people's views, and of societal forces (rather than personal commitment based on an individual's current liking or interpersonal attraction for the partner) and keep the marriage from splitting asunder.

As stated earlier, not only is commitment to marriage as an institution important, but spouses with greater commitment to their marriage as an interpersonal interaction and to their spouses as people reported fewer marital problems and less difficulty resolving problems when they do occur (Swensen and Trahaug, 1985; Rollins and Cannon, 1974). Those with a more personal commitment to the feelings of their spouses expressed more love for their partners and higher overall feelings of marital satisfaction, which did not diminish over time.

Our results underscore the importance of respect for and responsibility to (but not for) the spouse. *Intrapersonal fidelity* and *integrity* are also expressed as a sense of loyalty to the spouse and include the *expectation of reciprocity*. This lends itself to expressions of *trust* and *cooperation* and the creating of an atmosphere of *mutual support,* plus a sense of *accountability* to each other emanating from love and devotion. The overwhelming expression of *love* reported by respondents appears to result from their perception of being appreciated and valued by their spouse and having their needs met. A sense of *belonging* develops out of the positive interactions, and the possibility of continuous personal *development* becomes a reality as each spouse encourages the other to strive to maximize his or her potential. Individuation and familial cohesion are both encouraged and sought.

Good *communication skills* are the result of and simultaneously contribute to marital satisfaction and must be included in any list of "essential ingredients" of a healthy family ("Healthy Families," 1990). Respondents reported that communication occurs regularly and frequently. Openness, honesty, and *transparency in self-disclosure* characterize the interactions of satisfied couples. An assertive, clear disclosing of and sensitivity to thoughts and feelings, coupled with the utilizing of active listening skills by all family members, allows each to be aware of what is happening with the others. "Mind reading" is unnecessary. Communication is positive and affirming, with put-downs and other negative dispositional attributions conspicuous only in their absence. Appreciation is freely expressed.

The occurrence of extra- and intrafamilial problems is met with *flexibility* and a willingness to forgo personal gain at the cost of the other for personal gain only in combination with gain for the other. *Cooperation* rather than competition characterizes the interactions of satisfied couples, and solutions sought are win-win rather than win-lose or zero-sum. Good *problem-solving skills* are used routinely, leading to less impulsive or reactive decisions and better coping.

This freedom to call upon each other whenever needed highlights other essential qualities identified by participants: *equitable power distribution* and *shared leadership.* These couples reported their reliance upon *joint decision making* to resolve life's thorny issues. They heralded *compromise* and *creativity in handling differences,* talking through issues until a resolution satisfactory to both was reached. This did not preclude a clear delineation of roles among the contented couples, but did presuppose a flexibility in the expression of those roles as the situation warranted.

Healthy families and satisfying marriages are also characterized by *shared values,* either brought to the dyad by the individuals or evolved together over the years. A belief in something bigger than the self or the family unit that is worth committing oneself to was noted by many. This type of belief, often referred to as the *spiritual dimension,* was put forth by many respondents as an important aspect of the success of their marital union. The intensity of their beliefs on this issue was noted in the number of unsolicited comments jotted in the margins of the survey instruments. This sample, consisting of a higher than average percentage of devout Protestant Christians, may have a bias that would have predicted an emphasis on this issue. However, other studies of marital satisfaction (e.g., Fennell, 1987) with different populations have reported similar results. Clinicians should not fail to consider this aspect of family life (see Lewis et al., 1976, on the importance of a transcendental value system) when examining belief structures and looking for clues to motivations.

The final essential ingredient of successful marriages is the element of *fun.* These couples reported a strong, lifelong *friendship* (companionate love) characterized by the spending of enjoyable time together engaged in mutually satisfying activities. They related their appreciation of the sense of closeness and comfort with each other that had grown over time. They reported finding each other attractive and valued the *sexual aspect* of their relationship.

The results of this study have various implications for clinicians seeking to intervene with couples who have passed their silver anniversary, whether they are volatile (sometimes quarrel, but also remain passionately involved with each other), validating (compatible, supportive, and appreciative of each other), or avoidant (living parallel but separate lives while sharing the same domicile) (Gottman, 1994). In terms of basic characteristics of individuals who compose the marital dyad, those who were twenty-two years of age or older when they married, perceived greater parental marital satisfaction (and experienced years of modeling of a satisfying marriage), and are currently enjoying relatively good health and high socioeconomic status are more likely to experience marital satisfaction.

Although there is little clinicians can do about the couple's age at marriage (unless they are doing premarital therapy), the degree of parental marital satisfaction perceived, or their current economic status, they can help couples accept these facts, let go of anger, and adopt a more positive attitude. Furthermore, therapists can promote healthy lifestyle practices, assist patients in adapting to losses subsequent to chronic illnesses or fatal accidents, and suggest connections to community resources such as religious institutions or self-help groups that will enhance a sense of belonging and affiliation. They can also help to diminish anxieties and fears related to the aging and retirement processes. Since lower economic status does not in and of itself cause marital dissatisfaction, but rather is a mediating variable of stress, the introduction of stress reduction techniques and referrals for assistance with money management might be in order as well.

In terms of nurturing these essential ingredients, a commitment to remaining married may be fostered. The advent of a specific program of bringing pleasure to each other (such as Stuart's, 1980, "caring days") is in order. Concerns regarding interpersonal loyalty, especially in situations in which affairs have been reported, must be addressed (Kaslow, 1993). A sense of "we-ness" should be encouraged in the couple's thinking and speaking, as well as maintenance of their separate identities—being a strong "I" also. Good communication and problem-solving skills, including flexible thinking and cooperative problem solving, need to be modeled, taught, and encouraged, with specific activities prescribed to foster the acquisition and usage of these skills. Open discussion of power issues and decision making should be encouraged. Values clarification may help a couple to resolve many issues that arise from this realm of interaction. Clinicians might wish to suggest those community organizations most likely to be effective in assisting the couple to meet their needs and interests regarding values. Finally, it is important to encourage couples to engage in some activities just for fun—at a minimum, weekly, and preferably, daily. The review of a picture album from "the good old days" when their relationship was wonderful may rekindle memories of great times spent together and inspire them to expand their horizons as to what they can do together in the present to once again enjoy each other.

CANADA

Sample

The questionnaire was sent out with an introductory letter to 110 couples who had been married for over twenty-five years. Although most of the respondents live in the Toronto area, the study population was composed of people from different ethnic, racial, and religious backgrounds. Toronto is the most multicultural city in Canada, and its population represents a microcosm of the country's population. Since the sample originated through the families of students, it may overrepresent middle-class Canadians and underrepresent working-class couples.

Of the 110 couples to whom we mailed questionnaires, we received 71 sets back, only 69 of which were usable. All of the participants had been married between 25 and 38 years, with a mean of 30.5 years. The women in the sample ranged in age from 42 to 69 years, with a mean of 51.5; the men ranged in age from 44 to 73 years, with a mean of 55.1. A quarter of the sample (25 percent) was Protestant, 30 percent were Catholic, 11 percent were Jewish, 4 percent were Muslim, and 29 percent were classified as "other" (mostly Hindu and Buddhist). More than half of the sample (56 percent) described themselves as religious people, and about 44 percent considered themselves nonbelievers.

The study in Canada was conducted by Rena Cohen, who also contributed the basic data for this part of the report. Cohen is a professor of sociology at York University, Ontario, Canada, and specializes in family studies.

Most of the sample (77 percent) may be classified as middle to upper-middle class, while 23 percent of the sample rated themselves as working class or poor. In 54 percent of the couples, both husband and wife were employed. Of the employed wives, 75 percent worked full-time and about 25 percent work part-time. Among the men, 85 percent were employed and 15 percent were unemployed. The vast majority (96 percent) of employed men were working full-time. Men had more years of schooling in comparison with women in the sample. A majority of the sample (68 percent) reported being in good health, 28 percent reported that their health was not very good, and 4 percent reported poor health. The women indicated being slightly healthier than the men.

The sample was limited in several ways. As previously mentioned, it was not a random sample nor did it represent the entire married Canadian population. By selecting couples who were involved in long-term marriages, we probably ended up with a relatively traditional sample with a higher rate of ethnic and non-Protestant families than would be expected in the general population. Since the initial group of respondents was generated from among parents of university students, the sample tends to be biased toward middle-class and better-educated couples than generally expected in the Canadian population.

Results

Relationships in Family of Origin

Numerous studies have documented the impact of childhood family experiences on family aspirations and marital satisfaction in adulthood (Willette-Bloom and Nock, 1992). One of the general hypotheses of the present study is that adults who enjoyed close relationships with their parents and/or experienced a happy childhood are likelier to enjoy satisfying marital relationships in their adulthood than are those who did not experience a happy childhood and/or were not as close to their parents. Furthermore, it was hypothesized that individuals who perceived their parents' marriage as happy are more apt to enjoy satisfying marriages in their adulthood.

No one in this sample experienced a very unhappy childhood. In fact, childhood was described as very happy by 34 percent, fairly happy by 47 percent, and rather unhappy by only 19 percent. Almost all of the participants enjoyed a fair degree of closeness with their parents, especially with their mothers: 93 percent reported being close (59 percent very close and 34 percent moderately close) to their mothers, as compared to 76 percent who reported being either "very" or "moderately" close to their fathers. At the same time, most of them reported having little to moderate conflict with either mothers (78 percent) or fathers (67 percent).

Since we did not collect data on short-term marriages, it is not possible to confirm whether childhood experiences and closeness to parents really had an impact on the quality and duration of marital life. We can, however, conclude from this sample that most of the people involved in long-term marriages enjoyed close relationships with both their fathers and mothers. They did not experience many conflicts with their parents and had fairly happy childhoods.

Another interesting finding is the high rate of long-term marriages among the parents of the respondents. Parents' marriages lasted between 29 and 53 years, with a mean of 41.2 years, and only 6 marriages (4.3 percent) out of 138 ended in divorce. A solid majority of respondents (87 percent) reported that their parents had a happy marriage.

History of Marital Relationship

Most of this sample (71 percent) felt that their marriage was the outcome of their own will and free choice. However, 29 percent felt that they were coerced into marrying. Most of the arranged marriages occurred among Muslims, Orthodox Jews, and Hindus. The mean acquaintance period prior to marriage among the couples in this sample was 23 months, while the actual courtship ("keeping company") phase lasted an average of about 3.6 months. These figures are much lower than those from Israel (Sharlin, 1996, p. 233) or South Africa (Meyerowitz, 1996, p. 8), possibly due to the relatively high rate of "arranged" or "pressured" marriages in the Canadian sample.

This was the first marriage for almost the entire sample (99 percent). Age at marriage of the respondents ranged from 18 to 27 years, with a mean age of 20.3 years for females and 24 years for males. The marital age figures are lower by about four years (for each gender) than the general Canadian averages and may be explained by a higher rate of traditional ethnic families in our sample. The couples in our sample had 1 to 5 children, with a mean of 2.5. This figure is higher than the average for Canadians in general.

Dyadic Adjustment Scale

The mean score of the Canadian sample's scores on the total DAS is 107.4. In general, women scored somewhat lower (106.8) than men (107.1), but they did not differ significantly in the total adjustment scores.

Sense of Coherence

The self-rating instrument SOC was developed by Antonovsky (1988) to measure coping styles and to help individuals improve their health by increasing the ability to handle stress. This instrument, which demonstrated adequate degrees of validity and reliability (Antonovsky, 1993), has been used with different groups. The scores from the Canadian sample were higher than those obtained from a group of people who were brought up in a high-risk environment (Dahlin and Cederblad, 1993), but were comparable to those of social worker respondents by Antonovsky (1992) and in the Swedish portion of this study (Kaslow, Hansson, and Lundblad, 1994). The Canadian study of long-term marriages found very little difference in SOC between women and men. Similarly, there were no significant gender differences in either the Kaslow, Hansson, and Lundblad (1994) study or the "Lundby study" (Dahlin and Cederblad, 1993).

Causes for Staying Together

One part of the questionnaire inquired about the reasons for couples to remain together, even during difficult phases of their marriage. This question, in fact, offered the respondents an opportunity to explain the longevity and stability of their marriages. Table 4.1 displays the frequencies, in percentages, of the different motives for staying together. The primary reason given, both at the time of the study as well as during a crisis, was the lifelong commitment to the

TABLE 4.1. Most Significant Motives for Staying Together

	Now (%)	Crisis (%)
1. Marriage is a partnership for life	58	42
2. I feel responsible to my partner	41	20
3. I feel responsible to our children	25	33
4. We have children	13	20
10. I enjoy our lifestyle and do not wish to change it	20	
16. Love	36	23
17. Good, satisfying sexual relationship		
18. I believe I could not find a better partner in spite of a number of difficulties	14	17
19. We complement each other in spite of occasional tensions	13	7
25. One cannot give up easily on such crucial matters	10	22
32. I am convinced that we can resolve our problems	12	23
36. I still find my partner attractive	12	3
44. We have the ability to forgive	16	7

marital partnership. The second reason reason cited for staying together at the time of the study was a sense of responsibility to the partner, and the third was love. At times of crisis, the second reason for staying together was responsibility to children and the third one was love as well as the ability to resolve problems. There were no significant gender differences regarding motives for staying together.

Ingredients for Marital Satisfaction

Likewise, no major differences between men and women emerged when assessing the most significant ingredients for marital satisfaction. Women reported that comradeship, mutual trust, and love were the most important ingredients in their marriages, whereas men found mutual trust, love, and mutual respect to be most salient. Overall, for men and women, mutual trust, love, and mutual respect were the prominent ingredients of success. As to the desired components, the most desired elements selected were being patient and understanding, doing interesting things together, and being sensitive and considerate (see Table 4.2).

TABLE 4.2. Most Significant Ingredients of Marital Satisfaction (Canada, N = 69)

	Exist (%)	Desire (%)
1. Mutual trust	58	9
2. Mutual respect	55	12
3. Mutual give and take	39	9
4. Mutual support	46	10
5. Shared interests	26	10
6. Being patient and understanding	28	25
7. Respect for each other's independence	25	6
8. Openness, honesty, candor	26	4
9. Frequent exchange of ideas	16	22
10. Good problem-solving ability	12	12
11. Similar philosophy of life	16	9
12. Corresponding religious beliefs	19	4
14. Love	58	6
15. Loyalty and fidelity	35	6
16. Sensitivity and consideration for needs of spouse	16	23
17. Sharing leisure time activities	16	20
18. Mutual appreciation	7	10
19. Expression of affection	22	19
20. Consensus about sexual behavior	10	13
21. Mutual sexual fulfillment	20	22
22. Happy atmosphere	14	7
23. Doing interesting things together	10	25
24. Permitting each other individual development	13	4
25. Making major decisions together	28	13

TABLE 4.2 (*continued*)

26. Reliability	17	4
27. Financial and general economic security	23	20
29. Willingness to adjust and compromise	6	16
31. Shared interest in children	28	12
32. Avoiding repetition and boredom	12	17
34. Attractiveness of spouse	16	3
35. Fun and humor together	19	12
36. Mutual encouragement	14	10
37. Shared values	15	11
40. Feeling safe	23	9
41. Comradeship	43	23
42. Good listening	31	18

Discussion

This study investigated marital satisfaction among Canadians who were married for over twenty-five years. The results suggest the following: The top three ingredients for a long-lasting successful marriage are love, mutual respect, and mutual trust. These may be enhanced by similarities in background, common interests, comradeship, reciprocity (mutual give and take), and support. Identifying ingredients that are almost universal, or at least common to Western cultures, may be very useful in designing therapeutic models to work with unhappy and dissatisfied couples (Meyerowitz, 1996).

Another interesting finding which is corroborated by numerous studies is that men report higher levels of marital satisfaction in comparison with women, especially in the dimensions of dyadic satisfaction and emotional expression. This may be due to the fact that relationships are more salient in women's lives than in men's and they desire much more from them (Kaslow, Hansson, and Lundblad, 1994). Historically, men derived their sense of identity from their careers, for cultural and socioeconomic reasons, whereas women defined themselves in terms of their familial relationships. Thus, when things went wrong, women tended to be more interested in and more sensitive to perceiving relationship problems than men. In the same vein, feminist sociologists have observed that marriages, being usually nonegalitarian patriarchal unions, may benefit men more than women (Duffy, 1988). Thus, with the increase in both women's participation in the workforce and their sociopolitical independence, women have developed a lower threshold for marital imperfections and tend to be less satisfied with marriage than their spouses.

Couples in the study indicated a high SOC, which has been found to correlate with health (Dahlin and Cederblad, 1993). This study also documented that couples in long-term marriages score high on the Dyadic Adjustment Scale. While the two scales, SOC and DAS, covary, it is impossible to determine whether high scores on SOC (health) contribute to high scores on DAS, or whether high scores on DAS produce high SOC scores. It is possible that both scales measure corresponding factors and thus vary in a similar direction. The results of our study corroborate the findings of Sharlin (1996) and others connecting premarital family experiences and marital satisfaction. Most of the happily married individuals enjoyed positive and close relationships with their parents and perceived their childhoods as happy.

The most important contribution of the various segments of this international study on long-term marriages is the shift from focusing on the fragile and problematic aspects of marital life to the factors that make marriages solid, vigorous, and durable. These studies provide therapists with a set of ideas as to which elements are essential in long-lasting happy relationships. It is therefore critical that the findings in the study be translated into practical clinical tools. Since mutual trust, mutual respect, and love were found to be the top ingredients, it is essential to work on enhancing mutual trust and respect with couples whose marriages seem fragile. One approach to accomplish this might include creating assignments, role-plays, and behavioral scripts.

The results of the different studies have a great deal of commonality, which may indicate that the ingredients for a long-lasting relationship are rather universal and are not bound by culture or geography. Additional studies in different countries and subgroups are needed to further verify this conclusion.

Limitations of the Study

The respondent sample in Canada was small, nonrandom, and not fully representative of the multifaceted general population. Some subcultures, for example, Native Canadians, were not represented in the study. Also, long-term common-law relationships, a growing form of the family in Canada, were excluded from this study. The inclusion of these groups may have altered the results of the study. Furthermore, the study focused on middle-class Canadians and was less representative of working-class couples. Working-class marriages may last for reasons different from those given to explain the long duration of these middle-class marriages.

Another limitation was that the close-ended questions did not allow for a deeper elaboration of meanings. For example, what do people mean by "mutual trust" or "mutual respect" (not to mention the very elusive nature of the term "love")? Open-ended questions, or preferably semistructured interviews, could have segmented the term "trust," for instance, into several dimensions, such as financial trust, sexual-intimate trust, honesty, belief, and confidence. In a similar vein, "respect" can assume different meanings, such as admiration, consideration, deference, esteem, honor, or regard.

Chapter 5

Reports of the Western European Countries

GERMANY

The German portion of the study was conducted during 1992 and 1993. Data were collected from June to December 1992. The first version of the results was published in the German journal *Familiendynamik* (Hammerschmidt and Kaslow, 1995).

Sample Characteristics/Demographic Data

Our goal was to approach a nonclinical population. Criteria of participation were length of marriage and that both spouses were willing to respond. Friends, colleagues, ministers, and physicians from different regions in Germany were asked to deliver questionnaires to couples of different socioeconomic statuses. The other sample characteristics emerged coincidentally. While the religion of the respondents is close to a representative distribution, the level of education is high compared with the general population (see Table 7.2). The education level of men is significantly higher than that of women. This difference is typical for the generation growing up after World War II in Germany. The fact that only a few women work full-time has to be viewed in connection with the high professional level of the husbands and therefore, to their ample incomes.

The German study was conducted under the leadership of Helga Hammerschmidt, a psychologist-researcher from Munich, Germany.

To avoid unnecessary repetition, data for each individual country can be seen in the tables appearing in Chapter 7.

Relationship with Parents Before Marriage

Several studies support the influence of parents' marriage stability and quality on marital success in the next generation. However, further investigation has revealed that the effect of childhood relationships on adult mental models and behavior patterns seems to decrease in time (Hazan and Shaver, 1987).

Two results confirm the effects of the relationship with parents before marriage. For women we found a correlation between marital satisfaction and degree of happiness during childhood ($r = .36$; $p = .01$). Furthermore, the results show that women's marital satisfaction is higher if their husbands had favorable relationships with their mothers before marriage ($r = .23$; $p = .02$).[*]

History of Parents' Relationship

The following results show that the majority of parents' relationships were stable (95 percent). Furthermore, 68 percent of men and 81 percent of women evaluated their parents' marriage as happy. Eighty-nine percent of men and 85 percent of women remember a happy childhood. For 15 percent of respondents, the childhood was strained because of the loss of the father in early childhood.

History of Own Marital Relationship

The couples in this study had spent an average of 42 months getting to know each other and had "kept company" before marriage for an average of 30 months. A large majority (94.7 percent) of couples have children, and only 3.3 percent of their children were younger than 18 years. This means that the majority of respondents were in the empty-nest stage or the retirement stage (35 percent). When children leave home and job responsibilities diminish, marital quality tends to be more important for life satisfaction. Mean of marital age was found to be 27 for men and 24 for women. Only 14 percent married under pressure.

---

[*] This result is consistent with psychodynamic theory as well as with assumptions of modeling behavior.

Dyadic Adjustment Scale: Marital Adjustment

Lewis and Spanier (1979) define dyadic adjustment as a comprehensive, subjective rating of the marital relationship. The results of our study show that the means derived are close to those in Lewis and Spanier's sample and to the German sample of Hahlweg, Hank, and Klam (1990). This similar outcome confirms that our sample is consistent with the average population regarding marital adjustment (see Table 5.1).

The mean of dyadic consensus of the whole sample is rather high. There is no significant difference between husbands and wives on this measure. High consensus means few reasons for conflict. If conflicts do arise, they revolve mostly around: affectional expression, sexual relations, and, for women, particular habits of their spouse. It is not surprising that the level of conflict is significantly higher for dissatisfied couples. They quarrel especially about: affectional expression, sexual relations, philosophy of life, parents and in-laws, time spent together, leisure interests and activities, aims and goals considered important, and children.

Consensus can exist from the beginning of a relationship. The similarity concept is of basic importance in mate-selection theories. Yet, consensus can also be the result of mutual adaptation. We do not have information from our participants regarding this question.

TABLE 5.1. Dyadic Adjustment Scale and Subscales (Spanier, 1976) (Germany, N = 210)

	Women	Men	Spanier	Hahlweg
N	105	105	218	109
DAS total	114.44 (15.6)	116.56 (14.4)	115.00	115
Dyadic consensus	51.07 (6.3)	51.71 (5.9)	51.90	50
Dyadic satisfaction	38.64 (5.6)	40.45 (5.1)	40.50	41
Dyadic cohesion	16.37 (4.9)	16.23 (4.6)	13.40	16
Affectional expression	8.34 (2.1)	8.27 (2.0)	9.04	9
DAS 31	3.30 (1.0)	3.62 (1.9)	—	—
All Problem Areas*	85.11 (9.4)	85.95 (8.4)	—	—

*Dyadic consensus and eight related items.

Nonetheless, we are inclined to believe that the essential elements of consensus exist from the beginning and have ample chance to flourish during many years together (see Byrne and Murnen, 1988).

Dyadic Satisfaction

As indicated earlier, the concept of satisfaction is rather subjective. The degree of satisfaction depends on the fulfillment of expectations regarding the relationship. This criterion is essential when considering satisfaction as an outcome variable in the interaction process between the spouses. Table 5.1 shows the results on dyadic satisfaction for women and men. It is the only subscale of the DAS that shows a significant gender difference of medium size (d = .44; see Hunter and Schmidt, 1990). However, there does not appear to be a difference between women and men in the total score of dyadic adjustment. The gender difference in dyadic satisfaction is apparently compensated for through the outcome of the other three scales.

There are various empirically based explanations for these gender-related differences in marital satisfaction. For example, Harper and Elliot (1988) found that wives' marital adjustment was more affected by intimacy than that of husbands. Drawing from the German sample data, satisfaction as an outcome variable appears to be a function of all the resource variables. A consideration of these resources indicates the following: Based on the subscales of the DAS (see Table 5.1) there are no mean differences except for the satisfaction scale itself. In terms of couple resources utilizing the MASH Model (Olson and Stewart, 1991), it appears that men score lower in adaptability than women, although the size of this mean difference is very small (p = .01). The variable that shows a mean difference of medium size is problem solving (p = .01). This means that women do not see their interests and needs as being as well-fulfilled as the men do. Men are more successful in getting their own way and are less flexible. They generally get more and better support from their partners. A longitudinal study by Brandstädter, Baltes-Goetz, and Heil (1990) yielded similar results. Thus, there seem to be good reasons for men to feel more satisfied. In order to compare very satisfied and dissatisfied couples, it was necessary to define satisfaction groups as follows:

1. Very satisfied (mean satisfaction 41-43 and more), 20 couples
2. Midrange (mean satisfaction 36-38), 70 couples
3. Dissatisfied (mean satisfaction less than 36), 15 couples

With very satisfied couples, both spouses scored half a standard deviation (SD) over mean. Midrange couples scored half a standard deviation over and under mean. Among dissatisfied couples, one or both spouses scored more than half a standard deviation under mean.

In comparing very satisfied and dissatisfied couples, we find the expected highly significant mean differences of large size for all resource variables. Table 5.2 shows these variations between high- and low-satisfaction groups.

Marital Satisfaction As Outcome Variable in the Circumplex Model

Dividing the Circumplex Model (see Figure 2.2) into four general quadrants (instead of sixteen, as proposed in the original model) we obtained interesting results with regard to two different aspects. Since we are dealing with a nonclinical sample group, we can establish our study on a linear rather than a curvilinear basis.

TABLE 5.2. Mean Differences Between High- and Low-Satisfaction Groups (Germany)

	Wives		Husbands	
	very satisfied n = 20	dissatisfied n = 15	very satisfied n = 20	dissatisfied n = 15
Problem solving	43.11	33.47	44.30	34.67
Communication	44.63	32.60	43.90	32.13
Adaptability	38.40	33.93	37.30	33.07
Cohesion	46.25	37.33	46.85	35.80
DAS (total)	127.30	91.10	126.40	96.58
Dyadic consensus	54.59	44.24	54.33	45.95
Affectional expression	9.69	6.24	9.12	6.47

One finding is the clear confirmation of the hypothesis that couples rating high in both cohesion and adaptability are more satisfied with their relationship. The analysis of variance shows that group 3, which is low in both dimensions, differs significantly regarding couple satisfaction from groups 2 and 4, which are both high in cohesion. The best combination is high cohesion together with high adaptability, whereas the worst is low cohesion in combination with low adaptability. This finding clearly illustrates the great importance of cohesion for couple satisfaction. Although a high degree of adaptability is important for couple satisfaction, cohesion is fundamental. This finding was confirmed in the results of the multiple regression analysis (see predictive factors section).

Another outcome of interest is the cross-cultural aspect. In comparing the present sample group to Olson's (1988) national survey of "normal" families, with respect to the percentages of couples falling into each of the four quadrants, the following differences emerged:

- Quadrant 1: low cohesion and high adaptability—small difference
- Quadrant 2: low cohesion and low adaptability—small difference
- Quadrant 3: high cohesion and high adaptability— 6 percent less in the German sample
- Quadrant 4: high cohesion and low adaptability—11 percent more in the German sample

This means that the German sample tends toward the structured family type, as defined by the following four characteristics: leadership sometimes shared, stable roles, somewhat democratic discipline, change when demanded. This example illustrates the importance of being careful when comparing data cross-culturally.

Predictive Factors

To ascertain the best predictors for marital satisfaction in long-term marriages, multiple linear regression analysis (stepwise) was utilized. As potential predictors for couple satifaction, we considered all resource variables rated by husbands and wives, as well as biographic and socioeconomic data. The multiple regression analysis indicated that cohesion self-rated (beta .43), couple problem solving rated by husbands (beta .27), and dyadic consensus self-rated (beta .26) are highly predictive of marital satisfaction for women (R^2 .65); and that cohesion self-rated (beta .33), dyadic consensus self-rated (beta .32), couple problem solving self-rated (beta. 22), and communication rated by wives (beta .13) explain best couple satisfaction for men (R^2 .71). All betas indicated were found to be significant at p > .001.

Motives for Remaining Married

What makes couples stay together for so many years? Long marriages are not surprising when they have a satisfying relationship, though it is highly unlikely that such long periods could pass without crises. Crises provide opportunities and challenges for change and development. So the better question is: What were the motives of these respondents for staying together during difficult phases of their marriage? What were the attitudes, values, or special relationship skills that enabled them to pull through and learn from the crises? The following motives were highly rated by satisfied, midrange, and dissatisfied respondents. Thus, we can hypothesize that these are essential reasons for stable marriages, whether or not they are satisfactory.

Another question is: How do satisfied and dissatisfied couples differ regarding their motives? Table 7.7 illustrates these differences.

For numerous reasons we can surmise that, during the most difficult times of their marriage, couples have similar problems in and reasons for maintaining their marriage. Our results suggest that for those couples who are now dissatisfied, crises are not due to situational or temporal factors. It is supposed that their conflicts are also caused or exacerbated by either deficiency of resources or unconscious enmeshment. It is our belief that collusive couples can be found in this group (Willi, 1975/1990).

Ingredients for Successful Marriage

The most important ingredients of successful marriage for the whole sample are listed in rank order in Table 7.8. In the category of existing ingredients, the top three items for women and men are love, mutual trust, and loyalty and fidelity. There are only a few differences in the responses of women and men in this category, appearing mainly in the ranking of importance. It is not surprising that satisfied couples generally emphasize existing ingredients, while dissatisfied couples report more unfulfilled needs. Furthermore, it is evident that in dissatisfied couples, women and men do not agree regarding their desires.

Considering unfulfilled needs in dissatisfied couples, women desire sensitivity, empathy, and expression of emotion while men see consensus about sexual behavior as well as mutual sexual fulfillment as most desired ingredients of their relationship. The same variables appear as conflict areas of unhappily married couples. It is well known by marriage counselors and confirmed through empirical investigations that "women see sex as following from emotional intimacy, while men see sex itself as a road to intimacy" (Gottman and Krokoff, 1989, p. 50). Thus, it is not surprising that women's marital dissatisfaction centers on emotional issues, while men's dissatisfaction focuses on the lack of sex. This discrepancy causes misconception and tension. Although both partners wish mutual closeness, they cannot find togetherness in love.

Additional Analysis: What Changes Occur in the Later Years of a Marriage

An additional area of analysis focused on the changes that occur in the later years of a marriage. This question was considered using three factors:

1. Years of marriage
2. Age
3. Working versus retired status

Results

For the German sample, no mean differences were found regarding marital quality, satisfaction, or resources between the age groups. However, by analyzing the intercorrelations of the resource variables, certain changes can be observed. Obviously, some correlations change according to number of years married. Some variables become significantly more interrelated (p = .05) over the course of marriage. For women, problem solving increasingly depends on the quality of communication, whereas for husbands, problem solving becomes connected with marital satisfaction (see Table 5.3).

Another analysis was conducted on age, but no significance was found either for means or correlations.

Finally, does marital satisfaction change after retirement? Apparently it does. Couples are more satisfied in this stage of life. It was found that the mean difference in couple satisfaction for working and nonworking women is even more pronounced than for men. It should be noted that the group of nonworking women includes those who did not hold paying jobs for a long time, in addition to those who retired because of age.

TABLE 5.3. Comparision Between Three Groups on the Aspect "Length of Marriage" (Germany)

Years married:	Range	25-31	32-38	39-45
	Mean	27	33	41
Number of couples:		48	32	25
Wives: Communic.-Problem Solv.	Correlation	r = .70	r = .78	r = .93
Husbands: Dyad. Satisf.-Problem Solv.		r = .64	r = .73	r = .85

SWEDEN

Sample Research Group

Couples in the network of students in the School of Social Work at Lund University in southern Sweden, and others suggested by those respondents, were asked to participate. This form of network

The study in Sweden was conducted by Kjell Hansson and Anne-Marie Lundblad, both from the University of Lund, Sweden.

sampling, although atypical, was also used in the U.S. samples. It is a documented method for collecting data when a randomized sampling technique is difficult to utilize because lists of population groups are not available (Kuzel, 1992). We are convinced that this study population represented a good cross-section of the current population in Sweden based on comparisons with relevant official Swedish statistics. The way in which the study was carried out actually led to a relatively low attrition rate, as the participants were quite interested in the subject and outcome of the study.

The couples, all of whom had had a relationship for at least twenty years (married couples or cohabitants), were most often initially invited verbally to take part in the study. Once they had consented, questionnaires were mailed to 126 couples. Each partner was asked to fill in the questionnaires separately and anonymously and then to send the questionnaires (in a prepaid envelope) back to the Lund University School of Social Work within ten days.

Of the 126 couples to whom questionnaires were sent, 95 answered. Of those 95 couples, 5 did not fill in the SOC. Thus, there was a dropout rate of 25 percent. After we had started analyzing the data, three more questionnaires were received. Because they arrived too late, their responses were not included in the data tabulation.

Data Analysis

The mean age for women was 49 and for men, 51. The couples had been married or living together for an average of 26.3 years, with a range of 20 to 40 years. One couple had been married not longer than three years, but had been living together for 20 years before they married. One woman was in her second marriage. Ninety-two of the couples had children. The average number of children was 2.5 (a bit higher than the Swedish average, which now is 2.0). Some couples had as many as six children. Asked about religion, 91 women and 90 men answered that they were Protestants, while 1 woman was Catholic, 2 women and 4 men were atheists, 1 woman was agnostic, and 1 man did not state his religion.

The average income for 50-year-old men in Sweden in 1990 was approximately SKr 200,000 (median income was SKr 178,000). For women of the same age, the average income was SKr 133,000 (median income was SKr 129,000) (*Statistish Arsbok,* 1993). The income of those in this research group was comparable with these figures, which means that the study population is comparable to a national sample in this regard.

Sense of Coherence

The self-rating instrument SOC was developed by Antonovsky for researchers and clinicians to measure coping style so as to help respondents increase their stress-resilience capacity, thereby creating a health-promoting factor (Antonovsky, 1988). This instrument, which has shown satisfactory validity and reliability ratings in earlier studies (Antonovsky, 1992; Dahlin and Cederblad, 1993), was used in the research in Sweden as well.

Results

Dyadic Adjustment

The Swedish version of the DAS yielded statistically significant correlations, for example with Cronbach's alpha of .87-.93 (Hansson, Lundblad, and Kaslow, 1994). It was found that women and men do not differ significantly in terms of total adjustment. In the two subscales, however, the men scored higher than the women in dyadic satisfaction and affectional expression. For a comparison to the Swedish group, the researchers used Spanier's control group of married couples (Spanier, 1976). It was found that the Swedish values, overall, were a bit higher than Spanier's, especially regarding dyadic cohesion and affectional expressions. This may be because divorces are relatively easy to obtain in Sweden if people are not happy; the social support system protects women and children from loss of economical status; and little stigma is attached to being divorced, so those who do stay together are compatible and satisfied (Weitzman, 1985). To choose to live in a long-term relationship may mean that one is prepared to accept differences and to adjust to another person, which may not always be a positive thing.

In four of the thirty-two separate items, we found differences between the women's and the men's ratings. The men consistently demonstrated higher satisfaction (41.2) than the women (40), which was also true for the items that did not reveal any significant difference. The difference scales correlated with each other in an expected way.

Women's and men's SOCs do not differ significantly in the present "Long-term marriage" study nor in the Lundby study (Dahlin and Cederblad, 1993). Although the Lundby group had lower ratings than "long-term marriage" couples for both women and men, the differences were not significant. In comparison with a group of professionally trained clinical social workers, who also have high ratings in SOC (Antonovsky, 1992), the "long-term marriage" group had equally high ratings (see Table 5.4).

Comparisons Between SOC and DAS

The comparisons between SOC and DAS can be seen both as a validation of DAS and also as a hypothesis test whereby we are interested in the covariance between dyadic adjustment and sense of coherence. There were significant correlations between the SOC and DAS scores and the different subscales in DAS, both for women and men ($r = .53-.79$). Generally, those with a high sense of coherence also reported high marital satisfaction.

Discussion

In a mail questionnaire study such as this one, many factors can influence the result (e.g., it is probably rather easy for respondents to figure out how to get the most "favorable" score on the SOC and

TABLE 5.4. Sense of Coherence Mean Values and Standard Deviations for Different Groups (Sweden)

	Women		Men	
	N	M(SD)	N	M(SD)
"Long-term marriage"	90	153.7(19.4)	90	157.0(18.3)
Lundby study	83	150.8(24.5)	65	154.9(18.4)
Social workers	44	155.5(13.2)	18	154.9(15.5)
High school students (15-16 years of age)	148	133.5(31.3)	150	144.3(20.6)

DAS scales). Since the study was conducted as a "postal inquiry," there was no control over whether the members of the couple actually filled out the questionnaires together, even though the instructions asked participants to work separately and not to compare answers.

As far as could be ascertained, this was the first time that the DAS was used in a Swedish version. The researchers conducted a conventional test/analysis which showed that this version seems to have a satisfactory reliability when calculated for Cronbach's alpha. The different variables correlated positively, which could be expected. This was true both for women and for men. The results of this study also indicated that DAS seems to have a reasonable validity. The range of the subscales, as well as the entire scale, turned out to have a relatively normal distribution.

When interpreting the results, one must bear in mind that the study group was limited to couples who have chosen to remain married for a long time—twenty years or more. We have validated here that among this group of couples in long-term committed relationships, there is a high level of marital satisfaction, similar to that found in the American pilot study data (Kaslow and Hammerschmidt, 1992). This is in accordance with the expectation held by the investigators. Even if a couple has been married for more than twenty years, it is not a given that each experiences high marital satisfaction, though it might be assumed that this is the main reason for staying together. The range in the data analysis indicates that, even in this group, there is a minority of couples who report low marital satisfaction.

Gottman's (1994) research reveals that couples who stay together can be classified into three groups: (1) *volatile*—sometimes quarreling but also remaining passionately involved with each other; (2) *validating*—compatible, supportive, and appreciative of each other; and (3) *avoidant*—living parallel but somewhat separate lives and sharing the same domicile. We hypothesized that the high-satisfaction couples would fall into the first two categories, whereas the low-satisfaction couples, despite their tendency to become increasingly avoidant, would prefer for a variety of reasons not to separate, including fear of loneliness, commitment to the ideal of family, and mutual dependency.

It is interesting that the men declared higher marital satisfaction than the women on the variables that show significant differences. Indeed, on most separate items men rate a higher satisfaction level. There might be many explanations for this. Earlier studies have shown that men are generally less sensitive to relationship disturbances than women. When nothing in particular is amiss, men believe that everything is all right and therefore feel satisfied. Women have more relationship needs and desires than men do, which means that the relationship in and of itself is more important to a woman, while it is the result of the relationship that counts for the man (Lenneer-Axelsson, 1989). If we compared this group to women and men who had dissolved their unions, the results would have been quite different.

The couples in this study exhibited a very high sense of coherence (Antonovsky, 1988). In other studies, it has been shown that SOC covaries with health (Dahlin and Cederblad, 1993). The results show that DAS in long-term marriages covaries with a high sense of coherence (good health), but we could not discern which one of these factors is the most important one, as this was not a longitudinal study.

It could be of interest for more family therapists and psychologists to also focus their work on salutogenic factors (Walsh, 1982) instead of on factors that cause problems. It is important that these factors be based in current research. The present study is a step in that direction. In family therapy, it is often not clear which outcome will be best: divorce or a continued marriage. Many couples, however, seek therapy with the intention of staying in their marriage and making it better, or at least so they state initially. This research can possibly provide some ideas as to which factors are most salient to focus upon, namely, factors that create happier relationships.

In another study, thirty-five family therapists used a mailed questionnaire to explore the factors that couples thought contributed to a long-lasting marriage or pair relationship (Furhoff and Olsson, 1993). Most of the family therapists pointed to factors such as having made a conscious choice of partner, creating a home together, being able to solve problems in the phase of pair establishment, separating from parents, establishing individual private space, solving conflicts about finances, sharing the same norms and values about raising children, making time for shared interests together, having the capacity to see one another's needs and interests, and being able to deal with conflicts in a flexible way. This does not contradict our results where we have compared groups with high versus low marital satisfaction. The items regarding spare time, occupation, sex, philosophy of life, and quarrels seem to be what obviously differentiate the groups—that is, couples with high marital satisfaction show high levels of agreement in these areas as well. This finding regarding similarity of values, interests, and lifestyle preferences is congruent with the findings of Kaslow and Hammerschmidt (1992). In Sweden no differences were found between women and men regarding the importance of similarities in the aforementioned areas.

In line with the aim of this study, it can be concluded that DAS in the Swedish version is a useful instrument for studying marital satisfaction. Men's marital satisfaction seems to be higher than women's, especially when it comes to the dimensions of dyadic satisfaction and emotional expression. Women's satisfaction was most frequently contingent upon the level of their partner's satisfaction, according to a regression analysis. The same was not true of the men; their satisfaction was somewhat independent of the wife's satisfaction, deriving from other factors in the DAS subscale. Differences between them describing high versus low marital satisfaction were, above all, characterized by different points of view on issues such as spare time, occupation, sex, philosophy of life, amount of time spent together, and frequency of quarrels. The findings indicate a positive connection between marital satisfaction and SOC.

Clinical Implications

As a clearer profile emerges regarding the relationship ingredients that characterize satisfying long-term marriages, it is important that these be translated from research to practice. They can then be held out as a model for more satisfying relationships. The data reveal that trust of one's partner in all facets of life is a critical ingredient. Accordingly, trustworthiness and integrity should be fostered within the clinical setting. Sharing of values, interests, lifestyle preferences, and goals also emerge as an important dimension of fulfilling relationships. Thus, helping dissatisfied couples accentuate and build on what they have in common, while also promoting the need for some separate space and activities so as to remain separate and independent individuals as well as part of a couple unit, is another therapeutic goal. Other characteristics of satisfied couples include a sense of coherence (Antonovsky, 1992), having fun together, open communication that is tactful yet candid, good joint problem-solving and coping skills, a sense of commitment to each other and their family, and mutual respect and consideration.

These attitudes and skills can be highlighted in therapeutic and behavioral assignments, such as planning more fun activities, suggesting that the couple take turns if one tends to dominate, and providing the opportunity to deal with problem-solving challenges through role-playing. Clients also can be given articles to read about satisfying relationships in order to reinforce and help them internalize the concept of what constitutes a generalized portrait of a compatible, satisfied couple so that they have a clear sense of what they are striving for and some specific actions they can take to get there. This picture can be made more vivid by asking such questions as: What do you need to do to change your relationship so that it becomes more fulfilling (and less contentious)? What would constitute a happy interaction that is emotionally (and sexually) gratifying? A couple cannot reach a goal if they do not know what it is. This research is intended to help construct that goal—by establishing the dimensions of a broadly painted portrait of long-term satisfied couples that has goodness of fit and is applicable within and across diverse cultures.

THE NETHERLANDS

Sample

In the Netherlands study sample, the average age of the men was 60.7 years, ranging from 45 to 76 years, and the average age of the females was 59.0 years, ranging from 44 to 76 years. The average

---

The study in the Netherlands was conducted by Lore Finkelstein, Heemstede University, the Netherlands.

number of years of education was 14.0 for the males and 12.5 years for the females. Most of the respondents completed elementary and high school, followed by some professional schooling. Only 13 males (26 percent) and 6 females (12 percent) went to university. In regard to religion, the majority of the respondents were Catholic (41 percent), with fewer males (37 percent) than females (45 percent); 32 percent of the males and females were Protestant; none were Jewish; 5 percent adhered to "other" religions; and 22 percent declared themselves as not belonging to any religion. As for religious practice, 16 percent of the respondents did not answer. Another 78 percent reported being observant, while 22 percent were non-observant.

As for job and economic status, 32 percent of the males were working full-time, 10 percent were working part-time, and 58 percent were retired or not working. In comparison, 12 percent of the females were working full-time, 40 percent part-time, and 48 percent were not working or were retired. As for economic status, most of the respondents considered themselves well-off, as indicated by self-rating scores of "excellent," "very good," or "good." Among the males, 8 percent indicated "excellent," 20 percent "very good," and 56 percent "good." Similarly, 8 percent of the females indicated "excellent," 20 percent "very good," and 62 percent "good." Another 14 percent of the males reported their economic status as "fairly good," and 2 percent as "bad," while 10 percent of the females reported their economic status as "fairly good" and none as "bad." Regarding physical health, 71 percent of both male and female respondents reported "good" or "very good" health, while 28 percent of them reported "moderate" health and 1 percent "bad" health.

Relationship with Parents Before Marriage

When asked to give an appraisal of their own childhood, more females (38 percent) than males (34 percent) reported happy childhoods. On the other hand, 26 percent of the females reported rather unhappy childhoods, as compared with 18 percent of the males. Both males and females reported that they were closer to their mothers than to their fathers. In the "closeness to father" category, one response of "none" reflects the death of the father in the respondent's early childhood.

In terms of conflict, 20 percent of the males revealed having had quite a lot or moderate conflicts with their mothers, and 28 percent reported having had conflicts with their fathers, compared with 26 percent of the females who reported quite a lot or moderate conflicts with their mothers, and 28 percent with their fathers. Among males, 80 percent declared having had little or no conflicts with their mothers, and 68 percent few or no conflicts with their fathers, as compared with 72 percent and 79 percent, respectively, among the females.

History of Parents' Relationship

The average length of the parents' marriage was 38.9 years. One of the males' parents were still living, and three of the females'. Among the men, three sets of parents had been divorced, and of the women, two sets had divorced. Among the males, 92 percent of the parents' marriages had ended in death, 6 percent ended in divorce, and 2 percent were still living; whereas among the females, 90 percent ended in death, 4 percent ended in divorce, and 6 percent were still living.

Most of the males (60 percent) appraised their parents' marriage as "fairly happy," 16 percent as "very happy," 16 percent as "rather unhappy," and 8 percent as "very unhappy." Most of the females (54 percent) also reported that their parents' marriage was "fairly happy," while 26 percent reported that it was "very happy," 14 percent "rather unhappy," 4 percent "very unhappy," and 2 percent gave no response.

History of Own Marital Relationship

Nearly all (96 percent) of the males and females reported that they were married for the first time, with the remaining 4 percent in second marriages. One male with four children remarried after his first wife's death, and a second male remarried after his divorce. Only one couple did not have children; all others had two or more children, aged between 24 and 45 years.

The couples knew each other prior to marriage for an average of 43 months. Nine couples (4.3 percent) kept company or lived together before marriage for a period ranging from 2 months to 5 years, with an average of 15 months. At the time of their marriage the average age of the males was 26.2 years, while that of the females was 24.5 years. The average length of the current marriage was 34 years. Furthermore, 96 percent of the spouses declared that they had not married under pressure; of the remainder, 2 percent married because of pregnancy, and 2 percent wanted to escape from the parents' home.

Dyadic Adjustment Scale: Marital Adjustment

Satisfaction

In this study, males and females did not differ significantly in their way of looking at marriage and marital satisfaction. This finding deviates from those of other countries where males show more satisfaction within the marriage, while females tend to be more sensitive to relationship issues. One may take this as a sign of their common identity acquired during their years of togetherness. It may also be the result of a general change in attitude among men towards women's rights and their gradual emancipation (see Tables 7.10 and 7.11). In this Dutch study, there is also a minority of couples who report low marital satisfaction (see Kaslow, Hansson, and Lundblad, 1994).

Marital Satisfaction As an Outcome Variable
in the Circumflex Model

Both males and females chose as the most significant ingredients four items of the scale: mutual trust, mutual respect, respect for each other's independence, and mutual appreciation. These couples clearly believe that personal freedom is an indispensable issue for happiness in their marriage and they would not renounce it. They wish to maintain their own as well as their partner's personal autonomy.

Predictive Factors

In his psychoanalytically founded study of the dyadic relationship, Willi (1975/1990) points out the importance of an equal social-cultural background of the partners. Difficult problems may arise if the spouses come from different cultures or different social levels whereby they have been socialized according to different concepts of relationships. Willi (1975/1990, p. 15) suggests three principles for effective functioning of the marital relationship, which he has found, during his long years of therapeutic work, to be the most important:

1. A well-functioning dyadic relationship must have clearly delineated limits showing internal and external coherence.
2. Within the relationship, the spouses may assume a regressive attitude, i.e., a "care-asking" attitude, or a progressive attitude, i.e., a caregiving attitude, neither of which is limited to one of the spouses, but rather alternate in accordance with situations, assuring safety and solidarity.
3. Within the relationship, both spouses must have a balance of self-esteem that leads to mutual respect for each other.

Although the presence of these three principles does not provide any guarantee of marital satisfaction, they do constitute the framework within which a happy marriage is possible. Along this line, Minuchin (1974) and other American family therapists point to the absence of coherence, firm solidarity, and mutual respect as clear signs of disturbance in the family.

Most Significant Motives for Staying Together

The spouses were asked to select three reasons from forty-five items indicating why they had decided to remain in their marriage. For both spouses, the four most frequent motives given for staying together at the present time were the feeling of responsibility to the partner, followed by love, appreciation of closeness and comfort with each other, and that marriage is a partnership for life (see Table 7.7). During times of crisis, both spouses chose responsibility for their children, followed by feeling responsible to the partner, being convinced that they could resolve their problems, and finally again that marriage is a partnership for life.

Most Significant Ingredients for Marital Satisfaction

In this scale, the spouses were asked to indicate which of the forty-two listed ingredients presently exist in their marriage and which they would desire. They were instructed to choose a total of ten items in columns A and B. The results in column A show that both men and women chose the first four items referring to mutuality as the main ingredients for their satisfaction in marriage: mutuality of trust, respect, give and take, and support. It is noteworthy that there was no difference between women and men. In column B, the respondents were also asked to choose the ten ingredients that they desired in their marriage. The first four chosen were sensitivity and consideration for needs of spouse, sharing leisure time activities, mutual appreciation, and expression of affection (see Table 7.8).

One of the factors for satisfying marriage is that the couples are in agreement about the role that religion and the practice of religion play in their life. In former times the quest for corresponding religious beliefs between the marrying spouses was considered decisive, mainly by the spouses' families. Today there is a greater acceptance of intermarriage. Nevertheless, most couples belong to the same religion: the Catholic or the Reformed Protestant founded by Calvin. The latter tended to be severe in its requirements for daily life. On the other hand, the strictly prescribed way of life resulted in a high level of social consciousness.

In the scale that refers to the most significant ingredients for marital satisfaction, the choice of aspects involving mutuality gives a hint of what Willi (1985/1989) refers to when speaking of the intraindividual and interindividual balance. In both instances, mutuality guarantees the inner supports the spouses feel are necessary for a happy marriage. Here enters the factor of empathy—the capacity to make the other's concern one's own concern. Each partner is thus enabled to wholly understand and accept the other individual. It is also here that mutual understanding and support create the space where partners may find the opportunity to overcome traumatic experiences they suffered in the past.

Finally, it may be concluded that this study offers insight into the personality of those who have lived through the last fifty to seventy years. These people have experienced the impact of World War II and the postwar years with all the development and upheaval these have brought, and who have, within their marital togetherness, succeeded in adapting to a world quite different from the one of their youth.

Chapter 6

Reports of Israel,
South Africa, and Chile

ISRAEL

Sample

Two different studies were conducted in Israel, the first one on long-term residents and the second on new immigrants. Here the findings from the first study are reported. Of the 120 couples who were given questionnaires, we received usable returns from 50. Hence, for purposes of analysis, we refer to 100 individuals in our sample. All were Jewish and Caucasian. Women ranged in age from 43 to 70 years, with a mean of 58.7 (SD 7.9); the men ranged in age from 45 to 74, with a mean of 62 (SD 8.2). For country of birth, 50 percent of the men and 60 percent of the women were Israeli-born. The second largest group was born in Eastern Europe (36.7 percent for the men and 26.7 percent for the women); the remainder were from Western Europe, the former Soviet Union, and North Africa. Regarding the fathers' country of origin, we found that 60 percent of the women's and 56.7 percent of the men's fathers were born in Eastern Europe. Another 20 percent of the women's fathers were from the former Soviet Union and 20 percent of the men's fathers were Israeli-born. The remainder of both men's and women's fathers were from Western Europe. While more than half of the sample were born in Israel, nearly 30 percent immigrated shortly after Israel became an independent state (1948-1950). Fif-

The material on Israel is taken from Sharlin (1996).

teen percent were Holocaust survivors, all from Eastern Europe. No significant differences were found between these groups; hence they can be presented as one sample. The majority were of upper-middle-class socioeconomic status. Joint incomes between $41,000 and $50,000 were reported by one-third of the sample. Incomes of over $51,000 per year were reported by 60 percent of the couples, with 30 percent of them falling in the $75,000 to $100,000 per year income bracket. Thus, almost all respondents in our sample seem to have achieved a relatively high standard of living, particularly within the context of Israel.

All study participants were married between 25 and 40 years, with a mean of 34 years. Ten percent of the females and 6.7 percent of the males had married under pressure. Among males, 13.3 percent were in a second marriage, whereas all the women were in first marriages. Only one couple did not have children, while 80 percent had two or three (mean 2.5). Most of the children (83.3 percent) were age 25 and over. Regarding employment, we found that 74 percent of the males and 70 percent of the females worked full-time or part-time. In terms of religion, 78 percent of males and 82 percent of females indicated that they were not religious; this is higher than the proportion in the general Israeli society. The men had slightly more years of schooling than the women. The women were in slightly better health (68 percent) than the men (60 percent); 10 percent of the men reported that their health was not good. Finally, 70 percent of the men and 74 percent of the women indicated that they had happy childhoods.

Some Relationship Characteristics of Sample

Various aspects of relationships within the family were explored, such as relationship with parents before marriage, history of parents' relationship, and history of own marital relationship.

Questions about relationships with parents before marriage revealed that there were few differences between men and women regarding closeness to their parents. The men reported being closer or moderately closer to their mothers than to their fathers, while women were much closer to both their fathers (84 percent) and mothers (92 percent). When looking at conflicts between the couples and their parents, we see a reverse picture. More women than men have had conflicts with their parents. Two-thirds of the men have had few or no conflicts with their parents, while only half of the women gave this answer. Both women and men and show good relationships with the family of origin.

The average length of the parents' marriage was 34.3 years for the men and 37.7 years for women. Almost all of the men's parents were reported to be deceased (96 percent), while the women reported a much lower rate of death (82 percent). The majority of men (64 percent) and women (56 percent) estimated that their parents had fairly happy marriages.

The history of the respondents' own marital relationship shows no differences between men and women in terms of how long they knew each other. Both spouses reported knowing each other for 30 months and "keeping company" (spending time together) for 22 months prior to marriage. Men married at 26 years of age and women at age 22 on the average. A large majority of both men and women reported not being pressured to marry, 92 percent and 90 percent respectively.

Dyadic Adjustment Scale and Olson Scales

We found that women and men did not differ significantly in their scores on the total Dyadic Adjustment Scale. Women scored 106.9 (SD 13.8) and men 107.1 (SD 14.2). These figures are slightly lower than those in Spanier's (1976) original study, 114.8 (SD 17.8). No significant differences were found on the total DAS and the four subscales of it, as well as for the four Olson scales between males and females.

Motives for Staying Together

In our attempt to study the factors that lead to satisfied marriages, we asked our couples why they stayed together and what the crucial motives were during the most difficult stage in their marriage (see Table 7.7).

Table 7.7 reveals that in the category "today," love seems to be the most important motive for staying in a marriage. During times of crisis, the motive "marriage is a partnership for life" is most important for females, while males during crisis feel responsible for their children. The overall motives for the categories "today" and "in time of crisis" are totally different for males and females. More specifically, for some items, the mean number of males and females differed between the two categories. For example, "I enjoy our lifestyle and do not wish to change it" is cited by twice as many males in the "today" category as in the "crisis" category and by females three times more under "today" than under "in time of crisis."

Ingredients for Marital Satisfaction

The couples were asked to mark and rate the most important ingredients for marital satisfaction. These are shown in descending order in Table 7.8.

Very few differences were found between men and women; of ingredients that currently exist, for both women and men, top items included mutual trust, loyalty and fidelity, mutual support, reliability, and love, as well as making major decisions together. In the category of ingredients that are desired, we see significant differences from the first category as well as between women and men. Women indicated a happy atmosphere as one of the most important ingredients that they desired, while men cited mutual sexual fulfillment and consensus about sexual behavior.

For the whole group, there were again no significant differences between women and men, and the top ingredients mentioned were: mutual trust, love, mutual respect, and similar philosophy of life. Also at the same level of importance for women and men were mutual support; openness, honesty, and candor; and loyalty and fidelity.

Discussion

Generalizability from our findings is somewhat limited for several reasons: (1) Our sample was small and not representative of all the segments of Israeli society, thus not allowing some statistical manipulation. (2) The study was mostly conducted by mail, and even though our instructions asked participants to complete the questionnaire separately and not to compare answers before completion, the researchers did not have total control over whether participants followed instructions. After comparing each couple for differences between the males and females, we believe that our instructions were followed, as there is no evidence of combined work. (3) The questionnaires were much too long and we plan to shorten them in future studies. Some of the questions addressed intimate topics, which may have decreased the number of potential respondents.

The results of the study show that most of the respondents had good relationships with their own parents before marriage. It was found that two-thirds of the men and only half of the women reported having had conflicts with their parents before marriage. It may be concluded that the results reflect good relationships with the family of origin, and fairly happy childhoods. These findings are congruent with earlier studies. No marriages are happy throughout their entire existence. Raising children, illnesses and accidents, loss of family members, and other normal changes in the family's life cycle always require adjustments by each member of the family, as well as by the couple as a team (Kaslow and Hammerschmidt, 1992).

Conclusion

What characteristics actually keep married people together? All couples indicated love as the primary motive for staying together, as well as enjoying their lifestyle and not wishing to change it. The most important ingredients chosen by the Israeli couples were:

1. Mutual trust
2. Loyalty and fidelity
3. Love
4. Mutual support
5. Mutual appreciation
6. Mutual respect
7. Making major decisions together
8. Reliability

There were no significant differences between husbands and wives regarding the most important ingredients. Findings from this sample show a great deal of overlap with earlier studies, although there are some variations. Thus, the results reconfirm the basic characteristics believed to account for satisfying and lasting marriages which also include, in addition to those listed above, similarity and congruence of background including religion, education, lifestyle and philosophy of life; living in the present and future; and intrinsic motivation (e.g., love, enjoyment of lifestyle) as the basis for marriage.

SOUTH AFRICA

Introduction

This research attempted to explore the perceptions of couples who have maintained marriages for twenty-five years and longer in order to elicit characteristics and attributes that have enabled them to sustain their relationships through the stresses and problems which inevitably arise during a marriage. Additional factors researched were differences between the perceptions and experiences of males and females in terms of contributing to satisfying marriages, and comparisons between the respondents' marriages and their parents' marriages. The importance of this research is, therefore, to highlight the positive aspects of marriage, in order to help those working with people in unhappy relationships to discover possible untapped or hidden potential that may have been overshadowed by more negative feelings and behavior patterns over time.

President Nelson Mandela's "Rainbow People of South Africa" includes various population groups, most of whose ancestors have lived in South Africa for centuries. Others have descended from European emigrants who arrived after Jan van Riebeeck's landing at the Cape of Good Hope in 1652, coming from Eastern Europe, England, France, Germany, Holland, and Portugal. During the

---

The study in South Africa was conducted by Jacqueline B. Meyerowitz, a consultant at Family Life Centre in Johannesburg, South Africa.

twentieth century, new waves of immigrants have poured in from India, China, Greece, Hungary, Israel, Italy, Japan, Poland, Yugoslavia, and other African countries, including the Democratic Republic of the Congo. According to the South African Central Statistical Survey (1995), the estimated population figure for 1995 was 41,244,000, made up of 1,051,000 Asians (2.5 percent), 3,508,000 mixed descent (8.5 percent), 5,224,000 whites (12.7 percent), and 31,461,000 Africans (76.3 percent). The rate of population growth has declined from 3.5 percent between 1960 and 1970 to the present rate of 2.2 percent. South Africa experienced population growth of 22.8 percent between 1980 and 1990, that is, nearly a quarter in this ten-year period. It is estimated that more than half (66.3 percent) of South Africa's population is younger than thirty-one years of age.

South Africa is reputed to have one of the highest divorce rates in the Western world, allegedly one in three marriages. In 1995, the estimated specific rate of divorces per 1,000 married couples was 14.8 percent for whites, 7.8 percent for Asians, and 10.3 percent for those of mixed descent. The figure is usually not known for black Africans since the monogamous form of marriage according to Roman Dutch law is the only one recognized under South African law. Civil marriages in a court of law are open to all citizens. Nevertheless, forms of marriage that are traditional to particular groups continue to be contracted, especially African customary unions and marriage according to Muslim and Hindu rites. These marriages are still not recognized as legal, mainly because they are potentially polygamous and are not authorized by marriage officials. Many religious marriage officers conduct religious and civil marriages concurrently, which are then regarded as legal according to the laws of the state. Divorces according to African customary union or Moslem and Hindu rites are usually not recorded in state records. Nonetheless, however accurate or inaccurate the statistics appear, it is widely accepted that the divorce rate is high. Professionals from all walks of life—community leaders, ministers of religion, and others—are involved in working with unhappy relationships, marital breakdown, separation and divorce, and the resultant trauma experienced by all family members.

It is also recognized that the apartheid system of government, which was part of life in South Africa for several decades, and the transition period under the new government since 1994, has affected all citizens. Many couples and families have been affected by the exile and return of family members, the migrant labor system, emigration, hardship and death, insufficient education, malnutrition, poor economic conditions, and often an absence of parental influence. This last factor has led to a decline in family values, traditional values, and role adaptation, and, at times, an increase in role confusion among family members. For many communities the structure and values of the past have changed or are changing, and new structures and concomitant values are not yet well in place.

This research project involved couples who were generally in good economic circumstances, which means that few of the less fortunate participated in the study. If they had, the results would surely have been different.

Sample

The researcher for the South African portion of the study, Jacqueline Meyerowitz, is employed as a consultant at the Family Life Centre in Johannesburg, which is one of seventeen constituent societies working under the umbrella of the National Council for Family and Marriage in South Africa (FAMSA).

In February 1995, the members of the Professional Affairs Committee of FAMSA agreed to participate in the international research project on long-term marriages. A letter outlining the history of the project, explaining the plan for obtaining a South African perspective, and enclosing two questionnaires (i.e., for 1 couple) was posted to each society. The directors of the respective societies were advised to duplicate these questionnaires and to either mail or hand deliver them to ten couples. They were requested to return the completed questionnaires in sealed envelopes to the Family Life Center. The exact number of questionnaires distributed by the societies is not known, although in follow-up phone calls, it seemed as if most of them had contacted a limited number of couples and some had decided not to take part in the project. In Johannesburg, 120 questionnaires (i.e., for 60 couples) were either mailed or hand delivered by staff, counselors, and students to various recipients.

The questionnaires were distributed during April and May 1995. All societies were advised that a nonclinical population was to be approached and that couples had to have been married for twenty-five years or longer.

Finally, 91 completed sets of questionnaires were available for analysis, 51 from the Johannesburg area and 40 from the respondents approached by the other societies. Most respondents were English-speaking, white, middle-class couples, with only one Asian and one black African couple participating. Societies returning questionnaires were located in Cape Town, Durban, Benoni, Johannesburg, Kempton Park (National Council), Mossel Bay, Pietermaritzburg, and Welkom. The research will therefore provide a diverse picture, although the sample was smaller than anticipated.

Demographic Details

In this sample the average age was 58.4 for men and 55 for women. The average number of years of schooling reported by respondents was 15 for males and 13 for females. However, since mainly white couples answered the questionnaire and since other groups in South Africa have been largely disadvantaged in terms of opportunities for education, this statistic can only be considered as relevant in terms of the specific sample and can be generalized only to similar populations.

The majority of the respondents—49.5 percent of males and 47.3 percent of females—were Protestants, 20 percent of the females and 18 percent of the males were Jewish, 14.3 percent of the males and 13.2 percent of the females were Catholic, 2.2 percent of both males and females were Moslem, and 14.3 percent were classifed as "other." Some respondents did not answer the question relating to the practice of religion (8.8 percent of males and 12.1 percent of females). Of those who did, slightly more females (68 percent) than males (60.45 percent) were observant. It may be speculated that men and women of different religions married each other, as the number of males and females differed in Protestant, Jewish, and Catholic marriages. However, it should be noted that 95.7 percent of spouses followed the same religion.

Other shared motives to stay together included religious convictions and the ability to solve their own problems (see Tables 7.7 and 7.8).

Most Common Ingredients of Satisfying Marriages

Couples were asked to choose ten items from forty-two indicating the most important ingredients for marital satisfaction. The choice of the first five ingredients showed very little difference between males and females. In the column for existing ingredients, both spouses listed the same five items, with slight variation. The next five choices indicated some differences, with similar ingredients listed although prioritized differently. Men selected loyalty and fidelity and shared interests as important, while women included the similarity of religious beliefs.

Respondents were also asked to select the most desired ingredients for marital satisfaction. Ingredients most desired by men were sharing leisure time and doing things together, shared interests, sensitivity and consideration, patience and understanding, mutual respect, mutual support, financial security, exchange of ideas, mutual give and take, mutual sexual fulfillment, love, and a similar philosophy of life, followed by consensus about sexual behavior, permitting individual development, and openness, honesty, and candor. Ingredients most desired by women were sensitivity and consideration, expression of affection, patience and understanding, mutual respect, shared interests, similar philosophy of life, sharing leisure time and doing things together, loyalty and fidelity, mutual trust, and mutual give and take, closely followed by the need for financial security and openness, honesty, and candor.

It is interesting to note that ingredients most desired by males and females differ from the most common ingredients, and also differ between the sexes. One could thus speculate: to what extent do these couples share their thoughts and feelings about what they see as important and about what they need or desire for themselves and their marriages (see Table 7.8)?

The present results show that in 95.7 percent of couples, the partners have the same religion. This is in line with de Waal's (1990) findings that 85 percent of couples were married in a church, synagogue, or other religious institution. Willi (1993) states that people with similar backgrounds are more likely to have similar constructs and that individuals seek homogamy, that is, an agreement in cultural and religious backgrounds, tastes, and intellectual interests. A relationship of long duration denotes that two people are able to relate reasonably satisfactorily, and to this end there needs to be a degree of trust. It is therefore not surprising that the ingredient most valued by spouses in this research project was mutual trust.

Conclusion

What then keeps a marriage together and couples satisfied? Kaslow and Robison (1996) suggest an "underlying assumption" that couples who have been together for twenty-five years and longer probably "share a cluster of characteristics" (p. 154). Skolnick's study of marriages, in which she compares data from interviews ten years apart, found that "situational factors such as money, health and career success were of major importance in marital contentment or unhappiness" (Wallerstein and Blakeslee, 1995, p. 17).

In this study only 2.2 percent of couples described their economic situation as bad, which compares with the Israeli research results showing that almost all of the couples seem to have achieved a relatively high standard of living (Sharlin, 1996). Similarly, in this study only 3.3 percent of men and 2.2 percent of women indicated bad health. In her findings with regard to couples' health, de Waal (1990) concluded that the spouses who were more satisfied with their health were more committed to the growth of their marriage and had better marital integration overall. A further characteristic of satisfying marriages appears to relate to childhood happiness and relationships with parents. In this research, more than 75 percent of men and 83 percent of women reported a very happy or fairly happy childhood, and two-thirds of the respondents had little or no conflict with their parents. Wallerstein and Blakeslee (1995) drew the reader's attention to a good marriage as a unit that shapes adults and children and as such "more than any other human institution, is a vehicle for transmitting values to future generations" (p. 337).

The significance of similarity of background, including philosophy of life and religion, has been noted by many researchers. In his study of 147 couples in first marriages of over 20 years' duration, Fennell (1987) found "faith in God and a spiritual commitment" as well as "strong, shared moral values" to be two of the characteristics reported with the greatest frequency. Kaslow and Robison (1996) refer to "religious/spiritual orientation" as a characteristic of healthy families, although "there is no consensus regarding the particular aspects of spirituality that are important to optimal functioning" (p. 2).

The results of this research showed little statistical difference in the couples' marital satisfaction, degree of cohesion, expression of affection, and general agreement on lifestyle. There were also no meaningful differences in their ability to communicate, to be close yet flexible, and to solve problems. It may be assumed that persons in more satisfying relationships of long duration have been more successful in negotiating Erikson's (1965) stages of development and have reached a degree of "differentiation of self" (Bowen, 1976, p. 65), enabling more freedom from internal anxiety and more flexibility and adaptability to external stimuli.

It can therefore be concluded that satisfying marriages are partially predicated on similar shared interests in and responsibility toward the well-being of each other and the family. However, notwithstanding the many positive aspects of satisfying marriages, some in this sample did suffer from poor health, poorer economic situations, and more unhappy childhoods. In this respect, Willi (1993) offers the following reasons for some couples staying together: habit, comfort, fear of being alone, anxiety about change and uncertainty, and fear of losing social prestige and social security, as well as neurotic reasons. These couples are similar to the midrange and low satisfaction couples identified by Kaslow and Hammerschmidt (1992).

Clinical Implications

This research points to certain emerging themes that characterize long-term satisfying marriages. These themes could be regarded as goals on which to model therapeutic endeavors with dissatisfied and unhappy couples. The most important ingredient selected by couples was mutual trust. This suggests the importance of trust in a relationship, which is echoed in the safety and comfort of a therapeutic relationship. The most significant motive for staying together in these marriages highlights a sense of commitment of each spouse to the other, as reflected in the phrase "marriage is a partnership for life" even in times of adversity. The principle to be learned here is the importance of the therapist's commitment to the client, and how within the framework of such trustworthy and reliable environments the various issues can be dealt with, either individually or by the couple.

Within such a context, difficulties in communication, expectations, shared interests, basic values, mutual enjoyment, extended family problems, and parenting can be explored. Partners can be encouraged to express their needs and desires, to ask each other for help, to consult each other when decisions have to be made, and to find solutions to difficult problems. The therapist may follow the guidelines suggested by Wallerstein and Blakeslee (1995) in their nine life cycle changes or psychological tasks that are important for couples to negotiate in order to feel more satisfied in their relationship. In addition, Willi (1994) refers to the many phases of marriage, each of which varies in terms of intensity, intimacy, and motivation. He points out that each of the four phases has its own conflicts and problems, and that the transition from one phase to another produces feelings of fear which require a high degree of flexibility and adaptation from both partners. With this in mind, the therapist needs to be aware of the stages (phases) of marriage, to recognize the strengths inherent in each individual spouse, and to encourage and support the possible creative thoughts and plans introduced by the couple. Therapists may enhance the process by supporting tasks suggested by the couple and by recording the points made by the couple on a flip chart, thereby introducing a visual depiction of an issue. The latter idea increases mutual respect and sharing, which is modeled by the results of the research study.

CHILE

Sample

The average age for women was 57 (range between 44 and 77 years) and for men 59 (range between 49 and 78 years). Among the women, 89 percent profess some religion and 11 percent do not

---

The study in Chile was conducted under the leadership of Arturo Roizblatt, Department of Psychiatry, University of Chile Medical School in Santiago.

report having any religion, while 86 percent of men profess some religion and 14 percent do not mention any. Ninety-one percent of the couples have the same religion. Regarding education, 50 percent of the women have secondary or less education, 50 percent have higher education, while 18 percent of the men have secondary or less education and 82 percent have higher education; 36 percent have the same level of studies.

In terms of income, 45 percent of the couples have a family income of less than 6 million Chilean pesos yearly (US$24,000), 41.1 percent have an income between 6 and 24 million pesos yearly, and 14.4 percent have annual income of more than 24 million pesos. The individual average annual income for women is less than 6 million pesos, and for men it is similar to the family income of 6 to 24 million pesos. With respect to working hours, 79 percent of men and 23 percent of women work a complete shift, with a statistically insignificant difference. Another 5 percent of men and 47 percent of women do not work, with a statistically significant difference ($p < 0.05$).

As for their childhoods, 2 percent of the men and 11 percent of the women mention unhappy childhoods, with a statistically significant difference ($p < 0.05$). A statistical association exists between marital satisfaction and childhood experiences.

Characterization of Family History

In regard to relationships with parents, 27 percent of the women and 7 percent of the men reported significant conflicts with their mothers, as compared to 11 percent of the women and 5 percent of the men who mentioned conflicts with their fathers. It was also observed that 63 percent of women and 77 percent of men reported closeness with their mothers, as compared to 68 percent and 64 percent, respectively, who had closeness with their fathers. Regarding their parents' marriage, only 5 percent had separated. Finally, 80 percent of the women and 86 percent of the men described the appreciation of a good relationship between their parents.

Couple's Marital History

Regarding the relationship prior to marriage, 51 percent married in the first year, 75 percent within four years, and 92 percent within six years of having first met. Ninety-six percent reported marrying without being pressured. The average length of marriage was 32.85 years, with a range of 25 to 52 years and a standard deviation of 8.3 years. For 99 percent of the sample, this was their first marriage; only one man was married before, and his first marriage lasted for four years. The average marrying age was 23 for women (range 21 to 40, SD 3.6 years) and 27 for men (see Table 7.5). Ninety-one percent of the couples had had children, with an average of 3.9 children (higher than the national average of 2.5 children).

Marital Satisfaction

Concerning marital satisfaction, 80 percent of women and 88 percent of men reported being satisfied with their marriages. Another 20 percent of women and 12 percent of men were dissatisfied but stayed together. No important statistical differences were found between men and women, whereas statistically significant differences between satisfied and dissatisfied couples were evident, as shown in Table 6.1. In analyzing cohesion, for instance, we can observe a statistical difference in relation to working together on a project.

When analyzing expression of affection, we can observe an important difference related to the agreement between affectionate expression and sexual relations.

TABLE 6.1. Significant Differences Between Satisfied and Dissatisfied Couples in Different Areas of Living (Chile, N = 112)

	Satisfied (%)	Dissatisfied (%)
Often considered divorce	0	61
Regret that you are married	5	83
Don't kiss your mate often	10	61
Work together on a project	31	6
No consensus in sex	29	61
Handling family finances	50	11
Amount of time spent together	51	10
Personal attractiveness	44	10
Afraid to ask partner for what I want	15	39
Partner is not a good listener	6	39

In relation to consensus, there is a statistical difference between satisfied and dissatisfied couples in their resolution of issues about finances, recreation, friendship, philosophy of life, time spent together, home responsibilities, careers, alcohol, tobacco, drugs or food, and personal viewing of problems.

In terms of communication characteristics, important differences were found in the use of the "silent treatment" for dealing with problems, in the fear of expressing daily needs, in the satisfaction with communication, and in the expression of negative feelings.

Ingredients for Marital Satisfaction

It was found that the most important ingredients for marital satisfaction, for the satisfied and the dissatisfied alike, are love, trust, and loyalty (see Table 7.8). Differences were noted between the satisfied and the dissatisfied couples. Concerning the reasons for staying together at happy times, items of value and beliefs (e.g., responsibility to partner and children) are ranked highest, followed by intrinsic motivation (e.g., love), which is rated second. Both satisfied and dissatisfied couples included the following among their top reasons for staying together: "marriage is a partnership for life, crisis is inevitable, crisis promotes personal growth, responsibility to one's partner, and responsibility to one's children.

Motives for Staying Together

During hard times, intrinsic motivation, mutual support, and shared values and beliefs are the characteristics that link the satisfied couples. Also mentioned are: marriage is a partnership for life, responsibility to children, crisis is inevitable, the fact of having children, religious convictions, responsibility to one's partner, and crisis promotes growth (see Table 6.2).

Discussion

This research allows researchers and clinicians to glean information about couples from different social and cultural levels in an urban area, who have been married and living together for more than twenty-five years in a Latin American country. The majority of

TABLE 6.2. Description of the Motivation to Stay Together Now and at Difficult Stages and a Comparison Between Satisfied Couples Who Have Been Married for More Than Twenty-Five Years (Chile, N = 112)

Categories of Motives	Satisfied (%)		Dissatisfied (%)	
Stage	Now	Difficult	Now	Difficult
Values and beliefs	56	48	70	75
Intrinsic motivation	53	58	51	45
Mutuality	45	56	32	29
Extrinsic motivation	39	37	42	36
Social norms and expectations	38	35	30	28
Positive problem solving	35	30	23	32
Neurotic motives	5	5	6	6

couples can be characterized as being on the average fifty-eight years old and professing some religion. It seems that this element is very important in relation to the values and beliefs among Chilean couples, and it is also considered as a strong bond that contributes to the unity of married couples. The majority of the couples declared having had happy childhoods. The average length of marriage was 32.9 years, with a greater number of children than the national average.

In this sample, Chilean women have a lower educational level than the men, and half of them do not work. Most of the couples declared themselves to be happy and satisfied, although some of them rated themselves as dissatisfied. Since the dissatisfied are primarily women, there could be a connection with their educational level and the fact that they do not work outside the home or that they have a lower status than their husbands. It would be interesting to explore this issue in future research.

When analyzing the perception of satisfaction by couples, it was found that 88 percent feel satisfied. In comparing satisfied and dissatisfied couples on items appearing in the DAS scale, we found some statistical differences in the following items, which were mentioned more by satisfied couples: not regretting having married, willing to do whatever it takes to save the relationship, work together on some projects, can resolve financial issues, spend time together, personal attractiveness, communication. In the partially satisfied couples, the women expressed definite differences from those who were satisfied, giving less priority to loyalty and fidelity. Among men who were less satisfied, greater priority was given to mutual support in comparison with the more satisfied men.

Although some authors have criticized the usefulness of studying the subscales, the comparison of the results of the DAS with the samples from the other countries involved in this study is interesting, considering that in spite of cultural differences, there is much similarity among the studied groups.

In identifying the elements that motivate couples to stay together, a similarity can be seen between men and women, with the first priority being the conviction that crises are inevitable and that marriage is a partnership for life. This may be explained by the fact that Chile is a predominantly Catholic country, without a divorce law; nonetheless, similar responses were derived in all of the other study populations in which respondents were not predominantly Catholic.

Conclusions

As can be seen from the results obtained in the measurement of marital satisfaction, there is no statistical association between marital satisfaction and economic or educational level, with 36 percent of the couples having the same level of studies. There is also no statistical association between marital satisfaction and working hours.

While 11 percent of the women described conflicts with their fathers, only 5 percent of the men described the same situation. Likewise, 27 percent of the women described important conflicts with their mothers, but only 7 percent of men described such conflicts.

An association appeared between marital satisfaction and happiness during childhood. Only 2 percent of the men and 11 percent of the women in satisfied couples refer to unhappy childhoods, whereas 98 percent of the men and 89 percent of the women among dissatisfied couples mentioned problems during childhood.

In relation to their parents' marriages, only 5 percent had separated. The appreciation of good relations between the parents is described by 80 percent of the women and 86 percent of the men. There is no statistical association between the perception of their parents' satisfaction and the couple's satisfaction.

Due to the fact that in Chile no studies have been done on couples married longer than twenty-five years nor on the factors involved in their satisfaction, it is hoped that this present study, as part of the international LTM study, will establish a starting point in this area of research. The researchers (Roizblatt et al., 1999) also hope to find new strategies of support for couples who want to stay together and improve their degree of satisfaction. The results obtained to date must be interpreted with caution due to the small sample size.

PART III:
COMPARATIVE ANALYSIS
AND CONCLUSIONS

Chapter 7

Cross-Cultural Analysis

INTRODUCTION

Respondents in eight countries participated in the Long-Term Marriages (LTM) study. We are comparing data for several prime reasons. The overall purpose is to see whether there are differences between the couples in the participating countries. What can be learned from cross-cultural study for each individual country? Are all families alike? Are the factors in each country influencing the families in the same way, or are they different in every country? And finally, we hoped to be able to generalize and claim that, based on our findings and comparisons, the ingredients of LTM are universal. In accordance with our goal, the following topics will serve as a basis for comparison: (1) general family life characteristics in each country; (2) structure of correlations between family life characteristics in each country; and (3) factors influencing happy marriages in each country.

For comparative analysis, we used the structure of the research model as presented in Figure 7.1. The model should be read from bottom to top. One can easily follow the logic of the structure to see that the overall assessment of the quality of couple life is an outcome of the couple's resources, which are connected to the social and individual resources. The structure of the model, step by step, is presented in the Findings section.

This research has several justifications, as well as limitations. In terms of justifications, we can say that the same instruments were utilized in all countries, with the exception of the Swedish study, which used only some of the instruments while adding others (see Chapter 3). We therefore present in our comparison, in certain

FIGURE 7.1. Model of Research

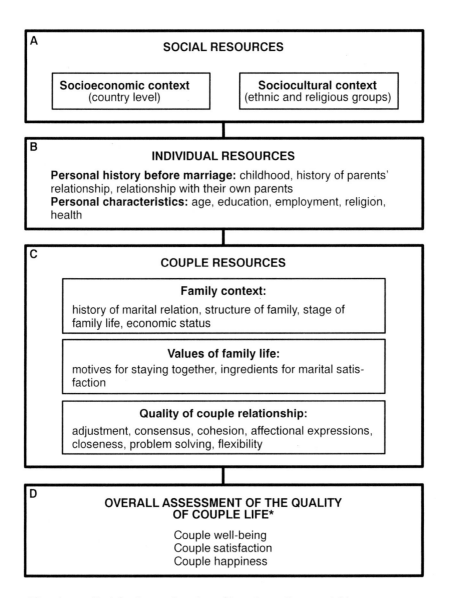

*See Appendix A for the explanation of how these three variables were measured.

sections, only the data from those countries from which we have full information. We fully recognize that the basis for any comparison must be use of the same criteria for selecting the sample. While these criteria were kept, there are minor limitations, such as the size of the sample, which varied from country to country; the number of participants ranged from 69 (Canada) to 210 (Germany).

The same qualifications for participation were used in seven countries, while deviations occurred in the eighth country, Sweden (see Table 7.1). The Swedish characteristics indicate differences in most variables including age, employment, and religion. Overall age is lower; more than half of the women and 81 percent of the men are employed full-time; and 95 percent of the participants are Protestants, which is almost more than double the other countries. It is important to note that generally the Swedish participants were younger, since the subjects were married for twenty years plus, while the rest of the studies used respondents married at least twenty-five years.

Some significant differences were found in Israel regarding economic status and employment. These differences are further explained later in this chapter. However, as will be shown, in spite of the differences in sample characteristics, there is full justification for the comparison.

One can deduce from studying Table 7.1 that no significant differences were found between the sample characteristics and family life characteristics in various countries. No significant differences in age and education were found, with the exceptions of Canada and Sweden, where respondents were slightly younger.

Thus, we may conclude the following:

1. Comparisons can be made between the countries, despite some sample differences, since the differences were found to be small and not very important.
2. There is no need to compare results in each country by age, education, etc.
3. Since no significant differences were found between males and females (see Chapters 4, 5, and 6), the couples were combined into one sample, which results in the N for each country.
4. The lack of need to compare the data according to sample characteristics is a major finding in itself, which lays the foundation for the conclusion that LTM is a universal phenomenon.

TABLE 7.1. General Sample Characteristics

Country/ Sample size	USA N = 114	Canada N = 69	Germany N = 210	Sweden N = 190	Netherlands N = 100	Israel N = 174	South Africa N = 182	Chile N = 112
Age/mean								
women	56.1	51.5	55.5	49.0	59.0	57.2	55.0	57.0
men	57.6	55.1	59.9	51.1	60.7	60.2	58.4	59.0
Education/years								
women	13.7		12.3	12.5	12.5	15.0	13.3	12.0
men	14.5		15.9	16.1	14.0	16.0	15.1	16.8
Employment (%)								
women:								
full-time	46	39	6	54	12	36	31	23
part-time	17	14	32	39	40	25	34	30
no	37	47	62	7	48	39	35	47
men:								
full time	61	82	63	81	32	40	77	79
part time	11	3	5	7	10	17	7	16
no	28	15	31	11	58	33	16	5
Religion (%)								
Protestant	80	25	47	95	32	0	50	0
Catholic	10	30	30	0	41	0	15	84
Orthodox	5	0	0	0	0	2	14	0
Jewish	5	22	0	0	0	98	21	4
Other	0	33	3	2	5	0	0	0
none	0		20	3	22	0	0	12
Religious (%)								
yes	89	56	80		78	18	98	88
no	11	44	20		22	86	2	12
Physical health (%)								
good	84	68	84		71	49	77	
moderate	14	28	15		28	42	20	
bad	2	4	1		1	9	3	

FINDINGS

Social Resources

To depict social resources, general statistics for each country are presented (see Table 7.2). In analyzing Table 7.2, significant differences between the countries can be seen. For example, income in the United States is three times that of South Africa. Differences can also be noted in the rate of marriage and divorce. As the various countries are different, it might be expected that these differences will affect other variables measured in this study.

Individual Resources

In this part of the model, the individual resources of couples in the countries studied are compared on the following topics: physical health, parents' relationship, relationship with own parents, and childhood. In each country, the participants were asked to rate their physical health as "good," "moderate," or "bad." There was a very low representation of "bad health," and two-thirds or more indicated "good health." Significant differences were found between Israel and all the other countries. Israeli couples have the poorest health, while couples in all other countries generally enjoy good health; the United States and Germany have the best. The poor health in Israel is explicable in light of the findings in a study by Sharlin and Moin (1997), who compared the data obtained from long-time Israelis and new immigrants from Russia to Israel. The reader will recall that in the Israeli study (reported in Chapter 6), a sample of 100 long-time Israelis was used. Our follow-up study included seventy-four new immigrants. These two groups were collapsed into one Israeli sample (N = 174). On most variables no significant differences were found. Nevertheless, comparisons indicated two major areas of dissimilarity: health and economic status. Findings showed that immigrants arriving in Israel were in very poor health and had lower economic status, due to unemployment. Their health and economic status affected the data for the entire Israeli sample. No significant differences were found when comparing long-time Israelis with their counterparts from other countries.

TABLE 7.2. Socioeconomic Context: Statistical Data

Country/Sample size	USA N = 114	Canada N = 69	Germany N = 210	Sweden N = 190	Netherlands N = 100	Israel N = 174	South Africa N = 182	Chile N = 112
Mean income (in U.S.$, 1993)	32,264*		21,250	25,000	16,294	19,095	12,789	
Quality of life index, 1985	98	98	97	99	99	96 9	66	91
Rate of marriage, 1993**	9.0	5.4	5.4	3.9	5.3	6.5		6.7
Rate of divorce, 1993**	4.6	2.71	1.93	2.48	2.39	1.39		.44
Mean number of children			1.67	2.0	1.53	2.38	1.3	
Marital status (age 50+, in %) married divorced	64.3 8.2		64.2 5.7	66.0 18.5	67.3 7.1	72.0 2.0	62.3 3.6	

Sources: Kurian (1991); U.S. Bureau of the Census (1996); Reddy (1996); Central Bureau of Statistics, Israel (1996).

* Median income.
** Rate per 1,000 population.

Results

Dyadic Adjustment Scale and Olson Scales

The DAS scale was used to measure dyadic satisfaction in the relationship (Spanier, 1976, 1988). The scoring of the variables was such that the higher the score, the better the relationship. The results showed no significant differences between men and women. On average, Women scored 106.9 (SD 16.4) and men scored 107.1 (SD 12.5) on the total DAS. Differences were found in the spread of the data among males and females, meaning that more males differed among themselves in their answers, whereas more females had similar answers in a given category. Scores on the Olson scales show no differences between males and females.

Motives for Staying Together

Respondents were asked to select three reasons from forty-five indicating why they had decided to remain in their marriages, both presently and in times of crisis.

At the present time. The most frequent motive given for staying together was that marriage is a partnership for life. Both males and females listed the same first four motives in the same order of importance, namely, love, not wishing to change their lifestyle, responsibility for their partners, and responsibility for their children. Thereafter, males indicated that shared experiences drew them closer and that there was no better partner. Females indicated closeness and comfort, as well as that shared experiences drew them closer.

In times of difficulty or crisis. Males and females chose the motive that marriage is a partnership for life first. Females then cited responsibility for their children, responsibility for their partners, that crisis is inevitable, that they could find no better partner, and that love and not giving up easily were important reasons to stay together in difficult times. Males chose the motive of responsibility for their partners, followed by responsibility for children, inability to find a better partner, the fact of having children, and not wishing to change their lifestyle as significant motives for staying together.

Although there is evidence of some variability on happiness of the parental family (see Table 7.3), with Canadians being the happiest and South Africans the least happy, we found no significant statistical differences. Regarding the history of parents' relations, the length of their marriages varied between 35.1 and 42.2 years. Again, no significant differences were found. When examining the parents' current marital status, we found that in most countries between 5 percent and 8 percent ended in divorce, with the exception of Sweden, which was a bit higher at 11 percent. With respect to the degree of childhood happiness, the comparison shows a very high degree of similarity (see Table 7.4) across the eight countries. A degree of similarity was also found in the relationship (closeness and conflict) with parents.

Couple Resources

Family Context

Couple resources included marital and economic status and history of own marital relationship. Comparison of the various countries on the history of participants' own marital relationships can be seen in Table 7.5. The comparison shows no significant differences among the participating countries. However, examination of the data again reveals the cultural differences between Sweden and the other countries. The length of relationship before marriage in Sweden was fifty-five months, and the cohabitation period, also highest among Swedish people, was forty-two months. It is interesting to note that the United States, Canada, the Netherlands, and Chile scored the shortest period of cohabitation before marriage.

Most couples were married only once (with the Canadian sample having the highest rate of second marriages, which can be explained as a sampling error). The Swedish sample had an average of 2 children, while Chileans had 3.9 children per family on average. Most country samples had respondents of middle- to upper-middle-class socioeconomic status, with the exception of Chile, where nearly half the sample had a poor economic status (see Table 7.6).

TABLE 7.3. Personal History Before Marriage: Parents' Relationship

Country/ Sample size	USA N = 114	Canada N = 69	Germany N = 210	Sweden N = 190	Netherlands N = 100	Israel N = 174	South Africa N = 182	Chile N = 112
Length of parents' marriage (years)	42.2	41.2	36.0		38.9	35.1	40.4	42.0
Parents' current marital status (%):								
married	17	21	9	19	5	9	9	23
ended in divorce	8	6	5	11	5	1	6	5
ended in death	75	73	86	70	90	89	85	72
Happiness of parents' marriage (%):								
1. very happy	26	24	21	25	22	9	25	83*
2. fairly happy	46	53	54	58	57	66	48	
3. rather unhappy	17	9	22	17	15	20	20	17*
4. very unhappy	11	4	3	0	5	5	7	

*Collapsed data: very happy and fairly happy (1 + 2); rather unhappy and very unhappy (3 + 4).

TABLE 7.4. Personal History Before Marriage: Relationship with Own Parents, Childhood

Country/ Sample size	USA N = 114		Canada N = 69		Germany N = 210		Sweden N = 190		Netherlands N = 100		Israel N = 174		South Africa N = 182		Chile N = 112	
	M	F	M	F	M	F	M	F	M	F	M	F	M	F	M	F
Closeness (%):																
quite a bit	53	32	59	32	41	27	48	38	38	22	53	32	54	39	65	65
moderate	33	46	34	44	48	40	37	55	44	41	31	37	29	37	34	25
little	11	15	6	16	9	17	15	7	14	28	15	24	13	19	1	7
none	3	7		7	2	1	—	—	3	5	1	7	4	5	0	3
Conflicts (%):																
a lot	2	6	1	6	1	—	8	7	8	7	6	9	8	5	8	7
moderate	19	12	31	26	17	12	37	28	16	21	23	22	26	20	9	56
little	55	52	48	41	54	48	43	50	52	48	50	38	46	42	21	11
none	24	30	20	27	28	25	12	15	23	21	21	31	20	33	62	26
Childhood (%):																
1. very happy	43		34		22				36		13		45		93*	
2. fairly happy	38		47		65				40		58		35			
3. rather unhappy	12		19		13				20		26		17		7*	
4. very unhappy	7		0						4		3		3			

M = mother
F = father

*Collapsed data: very happy and fairly happy (1 + 2); rather unhappy and very unhappy (3 + 4).

TABLE 7.5. Family Context: History of Own Marital Relationship

Country/ Sample size	USA N = 114	Canada N = 69	Germany N = 210	Sweden N = 190	Netherlands N = 100	Israel N = 174	South Africa N = 182	Chile N = 112
Length of relations before marriage (months)	35	23	44	55	43	32	27	36
Period lived together before marriage (months)	8	4	30	42	4	15	14	—
Marital age (years): women men	21 22	20 24	24 32	23 25	25 26	22 26	23 26	23 27
Length of current marriage (years)	35	30	32	26	34	31	33	33
Marriage under pressure (%)	12	28	14	10	7	6	10	4

TABLE 7.6. Family Context: Marital and Economic Status

Country/ Sample size	USA N = 114	Canada N = 69	Germany N = 210	Sweden N = 190	Netherlands N = 100	Israel N = 174	South Africa N = 182	Chile N = 112
Marital status (%):								
first marriage	96	72	86	90	93	94	90	96
second marriage	4	28	14	10	7	6	10	4
Number of children	2.9	2.5	2.6	2.0	2.7	2.7	2.1	3.9
Economic status (%):								
good	31	36			27	15	29	12
moderate	68	41			61	64	69	42
bad	1	23			12	21	2	46

Values of Family Life

Values of family life are characterized by motives for staying together and ingredients for marital satisfaction. The couples in the study sample were asked to indicate the most significant motives for staying together in their marriage. They were given a list of forty-two motives and were asked to choose ten, and then rank them in order of the first six motives (see Appendix B, Q.4 and Q.5). They were asked to do so for two situations: "today" and "in time of crisis." Results are summarized in Table 7.7. For a closer examination of these findings, we have prepared a series of additional comparisons.

Table 7.7 presents the most significant motives for staying together today and in time of crisis. The following three motives appear in the data for all eight countries: marriage is a partnership for life; I feel responsible toward my partner; and love. These motives rank as the first three in the category "today" for the United States and Canada, while for the rest of the countries they appear among the first six items, in varying rank order, with the exception of Chile.

In the category "in time of crisis," all countries ranked in first or second place "I feel responsible for our children." Thus, the partnership and the responsibility toward the partner, as well as loving the partner, seem to be the most significant motives for staying together. Love remains a motive both today and in times of crisis, while the most important responsibility changes from partner to children.

Additional comparisons among the seven participating countries on motives reveal interesting findings. The motive "marriage is a partnership for life" ranked first in the United States, Canada, South Africa, and Chile, while in Germany this motive ranked fifth, in the Netherlands fourth, and in Israel third. Germany ranked "attractiveness of partner" second and "good balance between independence and connectedness" third. The Netherlands ranked in third place "I have learned to live with a less than satisfactory marriage." For the category "in time of crisis," while "marriage is a partnership for life" was ranked first by respondents in the United States, Canada, South Africa, and Chile, "love" ranked first in Germany, and

TABLE 7.7. Values of Family Life: Most Significant Motives for Staying Together

Rank	Today								In time of crisis							
	1	2	3	4	5	6	7	8	1	2	3	4	5	6	7	8
USA N = 114	1	16	2	10	26	27	5		1	3	16	5	2	32		
Canada N = 69	1	2	16	3	10				1	3	16	32	25	2	4	
Germany N = 210	16	18	33	26	1	2	24		16	18	3	21	25	26	2	
Netherlands N = 100	2	16	34	1	10	19	3	18	3	2	32	1	14	16	4	18
Israel N = 174	16	10	1	3	2	18	27		3	1	16	14	4	19		
South Africa N = 182	1	16	10	2	3	26			1	3	2	18	16	5	14	
Chile N = 112	1	14	15	2	3	8			1	3	14	4	5	2	15	

1. Marriage is a partnership for life
2. I feel responsible to my partner
3. I feel responsible to our children
4. We have children
5. My religious conviction
8. Pleasure of our family of origin.
10. I enjoy our lifestyle
14. The conviction that crises are inevitable
15. The conviction that crises promote personal growth
16. Love
18. I believe I could not find a better partner in spite of a number of difficulties
19. We complement each other in spite of some difficulties
21. My partner has always behaved fairly even in crisis
24. We are prepared to accept the changes and challenges that make life exciting
25. One cannot give up easily on such crucial matters
26. Our shared experiences have drawn us so closely together
27. We appreciate our closeness and comfort with each other
32. I am convinced that we can resolve our problems
33. We have struck a good balance between independence and connectedness
34. I have learned to live with a less than satisfactory marriage

"responsibility for children" in the Netherlands and Israel. Comparison between "today" and "in times of crisis" shows interesting differences among the countries for specific motives (see Table 7.7). There is complete agreement among the United States, Canada, Chile, and South Africa regarding the importance of the motive "marriage is a partnership for life." The overall ranking shows great similarity between North American countries and in Israel as well, probably because of their great influence on Israeli lifestyle and beliefs.

The three most significant motives for staying together were: love, conviction (marriage is a partnership for life), and responsibility (responsibility for partner). As shown, very different motives were chosen by our couples in the comparison. Although conviction is chosen by most Americans, Canadians, and South Africans, love ranked highest among the Germans and Israelis, and responsibility among the Dutch.

Ingredients for marital satisfaction. Subjects were asked to choose the ten most significant ingredients for marital satisfaction, those which currently exist and those which are desired. Our participants chose different ingredients in these two categories. From the comparison (see Table 7.8), it becomes apparent that participants in almost all of the eight countries ranked love and mutual trust in the first two places, out of forty-two choices in the "exist" category. Also in this category, we can identify two additional ingredients that appear in all countries except Germany: mutual respect and mutual support.

However, completely different ingredients were reported when the subjects were asked which ones they desired. Respondents in all countries, except the Netherlands, chose "being patient and understanding," and "sensitivity and consideration for needs of spouse."

We analyzed the ranking order of couples in each country on the seven most significant existing ingredients for marital satisfaction. Mutual trust ranked first in all countries, with the exception of the United States and Chile, where it ranked second. The U.S. couples ranked in fourth place "corresponding religious beliefs," to which the other countries did not attribute any significance, while Netherlands couples ranked in third place "respect for each other's independence"

TABLE 7.8. Values of Family Life: Ingredients for Marital Satisfaction

Rank	Exist								Desire						
	1	2	3	4	5	6	7	8	1	2	3	4	5	6	7
USA N = 114	14	1	2	12	4	15	3	11	27	21	8	10	19	16	6
Canada N = 69	1	14	2	4	3	15	6	25	6	23	16	9	21	27	17
Germany N = 210	1	14	15	31	5	8	25	19	21	16	19	6	20	12	22
Netherlands N = 100	1	2	7	18	31	4	8	24	20	21	22	29	23	10	8
Israel N = 174	1	15	4	2	14	25	8	31	6	16	21	20	8	10	27
South Africa N = 182	1	14	2	4	3	8	7	11	16	17	23	6	5	19	2
Chile N = 112	14	1	15	2	4	6	11		6	1	17	5	23	32	10

1. Mutual trust
2. Mutual respect
3. Mutual give and take
4. Mutual support
5. Shared interests
6. Being patient and understanding
7. Respect for each other's independence
8. Openness, honesty
9. Frequent exchange of ideas
10. Good problem-solving ability
11. Similar philosophy of life
12. Corresponding religious beliefs
14. Love
15. Loyalty and fidelity
16. Sensitivity and consideration for needs of spouse
17. Sharing leisure time activities
18. Mutual appreciation
19. Expression of affection
20. Consensus about sexual behavior
21. Mutual sexual fulfillment
22. Happy atmosphere
23. Doing interesting things together
24. Permitting each other individual development
25. Making major decisions together
27. Financial and general economic security
29. Willingness to adjust and compromise
31. Shared interest in children
32. Avoiding repetition and boredom

and in fourth place "mutual appreciation." With the exception of the Netherlands, love ranked in tenth place, and Israel, where it ranked in fifth place, the first four ingredients were almost identical, although in different sequences, among participants in all countries. Analysis of the percentages for the top four ingredients that currently exist reveals that the first two ingredients in the United States were ranked that way by 81-82 percent of the sample—highest among all participating countries. There is a wide range in percentages in Germany, with mutual trust ranked as significant to 74 percent of the sample, while only 16 percent chose mutual respect. In contrast, a very narrow range in Israel, with percentages varying from 32 percent to 49 percent, shows that the four top ingredients are almost identical in their importance to Israelis.

Comparing the most significant ingredients for marital satisfaction desired by the subjects, it is interesting to note the differences between subjects from the various countries, who emphasize different ingredients in their rank order. For example, those in the United States ranked "economic security" in first place and "being patient and understanding" in eighth place, whereas both Canadians and Israelis ranked "being patient and understanding" in first place and "economic security" in sixth place. A possible explanation for the cultural differences may be the greater emphasis on financial well-being in the United States.

Finally, love was compared both as a motive for staying together ("today" and "in time of crisis") and as an ingredient for marital satisfaction (existing or desired) (see Table 7.9). In almost all coun-

TABLE 7.9. Values of Family Life: Love As Motive for Staying Together and Ingredient for Marital Satisfaction (Percent)

Country/ Sample size	USA N = 114	Canada N = 69	Germany N = 210	Nether- lands N = 100	Israel N = 174	South Africa N = 182
Motive —Today	57	37	56	34	42	36
Motive —In Crisis	30	24	34	20	20	13
Existing Ingredient	82	58	62	33	32	64
Desired Ingredient	11	6	4	17	20	15

tries included in the comparison, love is the most significant exist-ing ingredient for marital satisfaction—ranked so by a high percent-age; love is also the most significant motive for staying together today. Thus, it may be concluded that both motives and ingredients were viewed very much alike by most couples in all participating countries as contributing factors to LTM. This provides further validation for LTM as a universal phenomenon.

Quality of Couple Relationships

First the rating of the global Dyadic Adjustment Scale (DAS) in the various countries will be presented (see Table 7.10). The DAS, as was indicated previously, was designed for an overall assessment as a comprehensive and subjective rating of the couple relationship. There are some small but significant differences between the coun-tries. The normative global score suggested by Spanier is 114.8.

The comparison shows the following significant differences be-tween the countries in relation to the DAS (according to one-way analysis):

1. Chile, Sweden, and the United States have the highest DAS scores, with no significant differences among them.
2. Germany has a lower DAS score than group 1, with a signifi-cant difference from all the other countries. The German sam-ple came closest to Spanier's normative score.
3. Canada, Israel, South Africa, and the Netherlands have the lowest DAS scores, with no significant differences among them.

What can we learn from these differences among the participat-ing countries? The Chilean results are almost identical to those of Sweden, yet these two countries' cultures are completely different. One possible explanation is that in both countries couples showed high percentages of marital satisfaction (84 percent), indicating that they are generally satisfied with their marriages. The differences may be a function of the different religions and values in the two countries: Whereas 84 percent of the Chilean participants were Catholic, 95 percent of the Swedish participants were Protestants. In both countries, participants remained in their marriages but for different reasons. The Swedish respondents scored higher on the DAS, even higher than the U.S. sample, of which 80 percent were

TABLE 7.10. The Rating of the Global DAS and the DAS Subscales in Various Countries

Country/ Sample size	USA N = 114	Canada N = 69	Germany N = 210	Sweden N = 190	Netherlands N = 100	Israel N = 174	South Africa N = 182	Chile N = 112	Spanier N = 218
Dyadic Adjustment (total)	117.3	107.4	115.5	120.9	110.3	108.2	111.0	121.0	114.8
Subscales									
Dyadic Consensus	51.5	47.6	51.4	55.4	49.9	48.1	49.0	58.3	51.9
Dyadic Satisfaction	40.7	36.7	39.0	40.6	38.3	36.5	38.7	40.1	40.5
Dyadic Cohesion	15.8	14.4	16.3	15.8	13.0	15.0	14.8	13.9	13.4
Affection Expression	9.2	8.7	8.3	9.6	8.9	8.7	8.8	9.1	9.0

also Protestants. This might be due to cultural differences. In Sweden, it is rather easy to get a divorce because the social security system provides adequate financial support for single mothers and their children, which is not always the case in other countries. Furthermore, socioeconomic downward mobility is not as common in Sweden as it is elsewhere. Thus, the rate of cohabitation in Sweden is very high. Since women and children are financially secure, it is a common practice for couples to live together for many years without formally getting married. The Swedish sample included married couples as well as cohabiting couples.

When the four subscales (SS) of the DAS are compared, there are almost no differences in the first subscale, dyadic consensus, and no significant differences on the dyadic satisfaction SS. The visible differences observed while examining Table 7.10 reveal that the lowest dyadic satisfaction was found among the Canadian and Israeli couples (almost identical). For the dyadic cohesion SS, the only significant difference, albeit very small, was found in the Netherlands in comparison to the United States, Germany, Israel, and South Africa. The fourth subscale of the DAS, dyadic affection expression, reveals no significant differences. This SS is questionable in the literature (see Sharlin, 1996).

The next four scales, developed by Olson and others, were designed to measure the quality of the couple relationship. The four scales are summarized in Table 7.11.

As shown in Table 7.11, the Israelis scored lowest in all of Olson's scales. One possible explanation may be their correlation with three other variables in which Israelis scored lowest, namely: health, happiness of parents' family, and happy childhood. These variables are interconnected and serve as indicators of the quality of family life. Consideration must be given to the fact that most of these people came from poverty-ridden countries with a very low standard of living (either in Palestine or Eastern Europe).

No significant differences appear between the United States and South Africa in couple problem solving, couple communication, and flexibility. Significant differences were found between the U.S. and Israeli subjects in DAS, couple problem solving, couple communication, closeness, and flexibility, with the United States yield-

TABLE 7.11. The Rating of the Olson Scales in Various Countries

Country/ Sample size	USA N = 114	Canada N = 69	Germany N = 210	Nether- lands N = 100	Israel N = 174	South Africa N = 182
Couple problem solving	41.1	39.5	39.9	38.5	35.6	39.9
Couple communication	39.8	40.1	38.2	36.2	35.5	39.0
Closeness	42.9	39.4	42.8	39.2	38.8	40.7
Flexibility	33.9	32.3	35.3	33.6	31.1	32.2

ing higher scores. Significant differences were also found between South Africans and Israelis in couple problem solving, couple communication, closeness, and flexibility, with South Africans having higher scores. On couple problem solving, Israelis scored lowest among all eight participating countries. Couple communication and closeness were found to be lowest in Israel and the Netherlands, with no significant differences between these two countries. All other countries scored higher and with no significant differences. Flexibility was found to be low in Israel, South Africa, and Canada, while respondents from all other countries scored higher but with no significant differences among them. Again, the only explanation for these differences and for Israelis scoring the lowest on all four Olson scales may be the influence of recent immigrants from the former Soviet Union.

The reliability of the global DAS and the subscales, as well as the reliability of the Olson scales, were compared. The Cronbach's alpha results show that in both measurements, the reliability was very high and similar to the measurments suggested by Spanier and Olson, respectively. We do, however, raise some question about the reliability of the DAS subscales, particularly the affection expression SS (see Sharlin, 1996).

Overall Assessment of Couples' Quality of Life

In the final section of the research model, the overall assessment of couples' quality of life is presented first. Next, attention is focused on the structure of correlations and factors explaining satisfaction. Finally, there is a comparison between "happy" and "unhappy" couples.

The overall quality of life was assessed by rearranging the findings in categories to avoid the vague concept of "satisfaction," which includes two other concepts, namely, well-being and happiness. By separating the two, we may arrive at a finer distinction. The three measurements are:

1. Couple well-being—DAS item 18;
2. Couple happiness—DAS item 31 (see Appendix A); and
3. DAS subscale couple satisfaction, discussed earlier in this chapter.

Two other measurements will not be addressed. Table 7.12 compares all responses on "well-being" and "happiness." In all countries, well-being is significantly different from happiness. The greatest difference between the two measures was found in Germany and the Netherlands. The fact that there is a distinction between well-being and happiness may be explained by the hypothesis that one may feel well but not necessarily happy: people may think, "I am well due to internal and external circumstances, but not always happy."

Structure of Correlations

The tree of correlation (see Figure 7.2) represents a cyclic connection of twenty-eight variables presented in the six categories appearing in the following research model.

TABLE 7.12. Index of Couple Well-Being and Couple Happiness in Various Countries

Country/ Sample size	USA N = 114	Canada N = 69	Germany N = 210	Netherlands N = 100	Israel N = 174	South Africa N = 182
Well-being	.72	.45	.63	.60	.53	.64
Happiness	.48	.29	.19	.19	.25	.38
Delta	.24	.16	.44	.41	.27	.26

Social Resources

    1. Country
    2. Religion
    3. Religious observance

Individual Resources

  A. Personal characteristics

    4. Sex
    5. Age
    6. Education
    7. Employment
    8. Health

  B. Personal history before marriage

    9. Childhood
    10. Relationship with mother
    11. Relationship with father
    12. Happiness of parents' marriage
    13. Marital age

Couple Resources

  A. Family context

    14. Length of marriage
    15. Number of children
    16. Economic status (self-ratings)

  B. Values of family life

    17. Love as value of family life

  C. Quality of couple relationship

    18. Total dyadic adjustment
    19. Dyadic consensus
    20. Dyadic satisfaction
    21. Dyadic cohesion
    22. Affection expression
    23. Couple problem solving
    24. Couple communication
    25. Closeness
    26. Flexibility

Overall Assessment of Couple Life

    27. Couple well-being
    28. Couple happiness

Results have been combined from samples of only 6 countries participating in this study (Canada, Germany, Israel, the Netherlands, the United States, and South Africa), bringing the total sample to N = 849. The 28 variables were correlated, and Pearson's correlation was found to be g = .001. As illustrated in Figure 7.2, the most important variable is closeness (variable 25). Further anal-

FIGURE 7.2. The Tree of Correlation: Acyclic Connected Graph (N = 840, Pearson corr., p < .01)

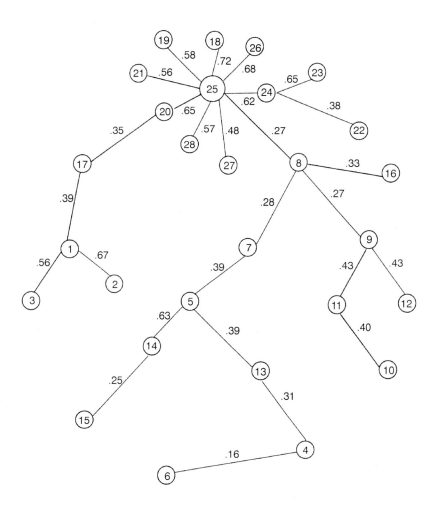

ysis of responses from each country showed closeness to be the most significant variable. The indicators of quality of family life cluster as a relatively independent system of characteristics, connecting to internal variables more than to external ones. Closeness, then, is the core of the system.

It can also be seen that there is construct validity for the research model. Figure 7.2 shows that variables (V) 1, 3, and 2 (social resources), are connected to quality of family life via love (V-17) as values of family life. Variables 10, 11, and 12 are connected to V-9, all representing individual resources. The connection of family background to couple closeness occurs via employment and health.

Factors Explaining Quality of Family Life

Dyadic Satisfaction

A stepwise multiple regression analysis was used to explain dyadic satisfaction as a dependent variable, using 22 independent variables:

Individual Resources

1. Sex
2. Age
3. Education
4. Religion
5. Religious observance
6. Employment
7. Economic status
8. Health
9. Happy childhood
10. Happiness of parents' family

Couple Context

11. Length of marriage
12. Marital age
13. Number of children

Quality of Couple Relationship

14. Dyadic consensus

15. Dyadic cohesion
16. Affection expression
17. Couple problem solving
18. Couple communication
19. Closeness
20. Flexibility

Values of Family Life

21. Love as motive for staying together today
22. Love as ingredient for existing marital satisfaction

According to multiple regression analysis, the following factors explain marital satisfaction:

- United States: 1. closeness (4.6), 2. couple problem solving (40), multiple regression (.74)
- Canada: 1. closeness (.59), 2. couple communication (.32), 3. childhood (.17), number of children (.14), multiple regression (.88)
- South Africa: 1. closeness (.30), 2. consensus (.28), 3. couple communication (.18), 4. love as ingredient for satisfaction (.15), 5. affection expression (.13), multiple regression (.76)
- Netherlands: 1. couple problem solving (.41), 2. consensus (.24), 3. dyadic cohesion (.21), multiple regression (.67)
- Israel: 1. couple communication (.28), 2. flexibility (.28), 3. love as ingredient (.21), 4. affection expression (.18), 5. dyadic consensus (.13), 6. dyadic cohesion (.13), 7. number of children (.11), multiple regression (.81)
- Germany: 1. closeness (.40), 2. affection expression (.26), 3. sex (.15), 4. couple problem solving (.13), 5. economic status (.09), multiple regression (.83)

The multiple regression coefficient shows that the ability of the variables to explain dyadic satisfaction is fairly high (.67 to .88). In four countries (Canada, Germany, South Africa, and the United States), it can be seen that closeness is the best predictor of dyadic satisfaction, receiving the highest score. What is also evident is that in all countries, *the high degree of dyadic satisfaction is explained by different variables of the quality of the couple relationship,* rather than by other groups of variables, such as individual resources or family context.

Global DAS

When performing multiple regression analysis by using global DAS as a dependent variable, it can be noted again that the variables selected have a high coefficient. According to multiple regression analysis, the following factors explain the global DAS:

- United States: 1. closeness (.61), 2. couple problem solving (.28), 3. love as motive (.13), 4. employment ($-.13$), 5. happiness of parents' family (.11), multiple regression (.82)
- Canada: 1. communication (.54), 2. marital age ($-.29$), 3. affection expression (.22), 4. religious (.19), multiple regression (.82)
- South Africa: 1. closeness (.40), 2. length of marriage (.25), 3. problem solving (.20), 4. flexibility (.17), 5. communication (.16), 6. religious ($-.15$), 7. age (.12), multiple regression (.78)
- Netherlands: 1. closeness (.41), 2. problem solving (.38), 3. number of children (.23), 4. length of marriage ($-.16$), multiple regression (.76)
- Israel: 1. closeness (.52), 2. communication (.30), 3. length of marriage (.13), 4. health (.10), multiple regression (.77)
- Germany: 1. closeness (.69), 2. communication (.20), 3. love as motive (.15), 4. economic status (.09), 5. childhood ($-.08$), 6. sex (.07), multiple regression (.87)

In 5 out of the 6 countries compared (the exception is Canada), closeness is the best predictor of overall dyadic adjustment. The figures are very high and much higher than for all the other variables. When comparing the differences between the respondents in each country, we see that different factors are important in each. For example, looking at the religion factor, in Canada the higher the religiosity ($\beta = .19$), the higher the adjustment level, while in South Africa the lower the religiosity ($\beta = -.15$), the higher the adjustment level.

Couple Happiness

Multiple regression analysis using couple happiness (item 31) as a dependent variable reveals different factors influencing this variable. One goal was to examine whether different factors also influence couple happiness and couple satisfaction. According to multiple regression analysis the following factors explain couple happiness:

- United States: 1. communication (.27), 2. closeness (.23), 3. employment (.22), 4. problem solving (.21), 5. well-being ($-.20$), multiple regression (.74)
- Canada: 1. communication (.52), 2. marital age ($-.30$), 3. religious (.20), 4. affection expression (.22), multiple regression (.78)
- South Africa: 1. closeness (.25), 2. flexibility (.23), 3. communication (.18), 4. love as ingredient of satisfaction (.18), 5. affection expression (.13), 6. number of children (.12), multiple regression (.68)
- Netherlands: 1. closeness (.48), 2. well-being (.23), 3. number of children (.21), 4. affection expression (.17), multiple regression (.75)
- Israel: 1. love as motive (.24), 2. closeness (.21), 3. affection expression (.21), 4. cohesion (.19), 5. number of children ($-.19$), multiple regression (.60)
- Germany: 1. closeness (.34), 2. affection expression (.30), 3. health (.15), 4. sex (.16), 5. economic status (.14), 6. communication (.13), multiple regression (.70)

In looking at the United States and Canadian samples, it is apparent that in both of these countries, closeness is most important for satisfaction, and communication for happiness. Couples in South Africa and Germany indicated that closeness is most important for both. Respondents in the Netherlands chose couple problem solving for satisfaction and closeness for happiness. Finally, in Israel, couple communication was given as the most important factor for satisfaction and love as most important for happiness.

According to the results of the multiple regression analysis, there are differences among the samples from the 8 countries in the list of factors and the level of their influence. However, when looking at what is most important in each country, we see *two factors that are common to all countries: closeness and good communication.*

Comparison Between Happy and Unhappy Couples

In Table 7.13, the ratings of the DAS and the Olson scales in various groups regarding marital happiness are presented. In all subscales, the highest scores were obviously found in the extremely happy group.

The motives for staying together in relation to marital happiness were compared between various groups (see Table 7.14). When looking at the motive "responsibility to children," we see that almost half of the sample fell in the "unhappy" group, compared with only 14 percent in the "extremely happy" group. In looking at "love," 62 percent were in the "extremely happy" group, compared with 14 percent in the "unhappy" group. Table 7.15 summarizes the findings on ingredients for marital satisfaction in the various groups. For the five most important ingredients, there are signifi-

TABLE 7.13. The Ratings of the DAS and the Olson Scales in Various Groups Regarding Marital Happiness

	Unhappy N = 43	Happy N = 191	Very Happy N = 168	Extremely Happy N = 161	E / U*
Dyadic adjustment/total	90.1	104.4	104.4	122.0	1.4
Subscales of DAS:					
Dyadic consensus	42.5	47.5	50.3	52.7	1.2
Dyadic cohesion	10.9	13.2	15.8	16.6	1.5
Dyadic expression	7.4	8.2	9.0	9.9	1.3
Olson Scales					
Couple problem solving	30.9	36.6	39.7	41.7	1.4
Couple communication	29.2	34.8	39.5	41.2	1.4
Closeness	31.3	37.3	42.4	44.4	1.4
Flexibility	26.0	30.9	33.9	35.6	1.4

* Ratio = extreme marital happiness/marital unhappiness

TABLE 7.14. Motives for Staying Together in Various Groups (Percent)

	Unhappy N = 43	Happy N = 191	Very Happy N = 168	Extremely Happy N = 161	Δ
Responsible to children	42	21	21	14	-28
Lifestyle	16	28	36	31	15
Love	14	29	42	62	49

Δ = Extremely happy - unhappy

TABLE 7.15. Ingredients for Marital Satisfaction in Various Groups (Percent)

	Unhappy N = 43	Happy N = 191	Very Happy N = 168	Extremely Happy N = 161	Δ
Mutual trust	49	64	71	74	25
Mutual respect	30	54	60	63	33
Mutual support	33	44	45	57	24
Openness	26	31	43	42	16
Love	26	33	63	72	46

Δ = Extremely happy - unhappy

cant differences between the groups, with the highest difference for "love" (62 percent) in the "extremely happy" group.

Psychological Aspects of Love

The data imply that fulfillment in love is perceived as the source of greatest happiness, and thus disappointment in love may lead to deep despair. Why is love so important? Being loved shows us that we are special for another individual. The affection displayed by the person we love strengthens our self-esteem. Fulfilled love satisfies the yearning for security and caring, from which one gains strength. In addition, the meaning of love goes beyond the boundary between I and you. A successful relationship between husband and wife is the nucleus of love. It holds the family together and is handed down from generation to generation—unfortunately, with all its unsatisfactory aspects as well. Internalized love enables us to develop the ability to turn to others with respect, attention, and support. When we are satisfied with our love, we are peaceful. The family shares a common destiny. Because love is an indispensable basic need, lack of love must have severe consequences for the succeeding generation. Lack of security leads to alienation. Inner emptiness expresses itself in boredom and indifference. The desperation arising from empty relationships may lead adolescents to violent and self-destructive behaviors.

For thousands of years, the major religions and schools of philosophy have taught that love is a power for good. The ideal of love is viewed as an internalized principle. Yet, it will never be possible to grasp the phenomenon of love in all of its layers and complexity and with all of its individual aspects. How can we ever be certain that love means the same thing to everyone? Fortunately, there seems to be wide agreement that a number of elements are more or less essential to the nature of love. Maxwell (1985) found that most people regard three elements as indispensable to a loving partnership:

- Closeness/intimacy
- Passion
- Commitment

These three components are supported by theoretical studies (Sternberg, 1988) and confirmed by empirical investigations. Branden (1988, p. 220) defines romantic love as "a passionate spiritual-emotional-sexual attachment between two people that reflects a high regard for the value of each other's person." Love, in this sense, encompasses the entire human being. Although the term love is clearly associated with various kinds of experience, it must nevertheless be seen as a holistic phenomenon. Erotic love implies an intimate integration of body and soul. If we are to achieve a clearer understanding of love, however, we must treat separately the three elements that have been designated its components.

The first phase of a relationship is often characterized by physical attraction and can quickly develop into *passion*. Although the sexual element plays a central role in such a relationship, other basic needs are also involved, including the need for human companionship, self-awareness, self-discovery, and dominance. Passion tends to ignite suddenly and is the least constant aspect of love. However, although physical attraction may decline with time, it does not necessarily disappear irrevocably during the course of a long relationship. This somewhat inconstant aspect of love contrasts with the component of closeness/intimacy, which may be more enduring.

Closeness "refers to close, connected and bonded feelings in loving relationships" (Sternberg, 1988, p. 120). "*Intimacy* is characterized as the subjective side of relatedness, the sharing of personal feelings, fantasies and affectively meaningful experience" (Wynne, 1988, p. 95). Closeness and intimacy generally develop slowly. If love is to endure over the long term, it must be sustained by such emotional affinity as passion cools. Whereas passion arises spontaneously and may well vanish just as quickly, intimacy must be established and nurtured carefully. "This process includes emotionally charged verbal or non-verbal self-disclosure of a kind that connotes an acceptance by the listener who could betray or exploit the speaker, but who is trusted not to do so. This definition suggests that intimacy can be a deeply powerful, meaningful, and humanizing experience, subtly and emotionally complicated, seductive but frightening" (Wynne, 1988, p. 95). When we accept our own vulnerability and trust that our partner will understand and accept us in all our candid individuality, we create a unique opportunity to see ourselves with the other's eyes. Seeking each other and revealing ourselves to each other in a loving spirit promotes self-realization and maturation. Such intimacy is so difficult to achieve precisely because it unavoidably forces us to face our fears and vulnerability too. It requires the greatest circumspection and will always fall short of reaching the innermost core of the other, even under the most ideal circumstances. However, mutual trust and concern ensure the continued flow of communication. The essential point is that we relate to each other in an attentive, empathic, and supportive way from the very beginning of the relationship and throughout its existence.

Commitment refers to the desire to maintain a relationship that motivates us to make the necessary effort to be mindful and responsible. It implies the willingness to persevere and the awareness of a mutual affection that leads to the wish to stay "together through thick and thin." However, it should be stressed that commitment does *not* mean staying in a marriage which has irreparably failed. A loveless, dogmatic insistence on maintaining the marriage can produce a living hell in which both partners suffocate.

Couples who have been together for a long time indicate that no relationship is without its ups and downs. Individual development and the trials and tribulations of everyday life are bound to engender tensions. Problems have to be faced and resolved. However, the willingness to stay together leads to an inner conviction that provides the key to mastering these difficulties. Many admit that their love has grown deeper after crises have been successfully traversed. It is through meeting such challenges that partners develop fairness and patience in relating to each other. "The course of the commitment dimension of love over the duration of marriage depends in large part upon the success of that relationship and vice versa" (Sternberg, 1988, p. 132). Although the intensity of love may already be discernible at the beginning of a relationship, real depth of love is reached only through a relationship forged in the kiln of time. Such depth is not easily acquired, but is rather the result of unflagging mutual effort. It might be added that contemporary society offers little encouragement to attempt long-term commitment because of its strong emphasis on egoistic gratification. Impatience and unwillingness to deal with conflicts, together with growing personal ambitions, are obstacles to developing a successful in-depth relationship.

There can be no doubt, as the results of this study confirm, that favorable conditions experienced during childhood in a loving home build up a stable basis of trust that forms the fundamental prerequisite for all intimate relationships in later life. The patterns of behavior and the values that individuals have witnessed influence relationships throughout their lives. However, it is never too late for change, particularly as far as love is concerned. Through positive experiences in a partnership or with the assistance of a competent therapist, one can overcome prejudices, compensate for deficits originating in childhood, and even heal old wounds.

Love comes in a variety of forms according to different combinations of the three components. Each individual experiences the three dimensions of love, namely passion, intimacy, and commitment, to varying degrees of intensity. However, love is not determined only by the intensity of its three basic dimensions, but also acquires a special character by virtue of individual traits. Thus, love appears in many guises, depending on the dispositions of the individuals. Since individuals change over the course of time, it is quite natural for the essence of love in a relationship to change over the years. The decisive feature is that the vital needs of both partners are fulfilled and the balance between them is reestablished again and again. "A perfectly good relationship may be destroyed for lack of knowledge about the nature of intimate involvement in close relationships" (Sternberg, 1986, p.126).

Surveys have shown that with the multitude of combinations, six different types of love are found. Lee (1988) calls these variations the *colors of love:*

1. *Erotic love* always begins with strong physical attraction. However, erotic appeal does not depend on sexual attraction alone; it responds no less to certain desirable personality traits. If love at first sight is not just a transient gust of excitement, then the partners can succeed in creating a stable and fulfilling relationship. Various studies have found that erotic partnerships with their sensual joys are the happiest, irrespective of the duration of the relationship or the age of the partners.

2. *Companionate love,* on the other hand, is a deeply committed and intimate relationship in which passion may play a lesser role. Companionate love frequently grows out of a close friendship in which the partners already know each other well. The relationship is based on similar attitudes and interests.

3. *Passionate love* is always possessive. The passion is ego-centered and stirs up intense feelings. Lovers with this orientation also have a tendency to be doubtful and jealous.

4. *Pragmatic love* is hardly passionate at all. Its principal element is reason. The partners are linked by similar goals and practi-

cal considerations. This kind of love does not excite but is very rational.

5. *Altruistic love* prevails when the actions of each partner are strongly oriented to the well-being of the other. Giving means joy and enrichment rather than sacrifice. If both partners live by these principles, then their relationship will be characterized by loving care and good communication.

6. *Playful love* is not love in the true sense, since those who indulge in it do not take feelings seriously and shun commitment. They typically play the game of seduction and sexual adventure. When only one partner has this tendency, the relationship is usually very unhappy.

The greatest agreement between the partners in their attitude toward love is found in erotic, altrustic, and pragmatic partnerships. Although erotic relationships are the happiest, those couples who are attached to each other in loving, mutual care also experience happiness and satisfaction. *A personal style of love tends to be a blend of various attitudes.* This blend also determines how well two people are suited to each other. Sexual pair-bonds differ from other important loving relationships because it creates a craving for greater closeness in other life domains, which makes marital love exclusive.

In relationships of long duration, the romantic elements tend to ebb with time, giving way to a more altruistic, companionate, or pragmatic partnership. This study clearly shows the exceptional importance of love in a marriage lasting many years. Indeed, love was most frequently mentioned as the reason for the success of a marriage. In addition, the preferred ingredients for marital satisfaction reaffirmed the clear avowal of love: mutual trust, closeness, mutual respect, commitment, responsibility, and the desire for togetherness.

A couple's shared history is particularly important for love in the later phases of life. Emotions, both positive and negative, tend to become more intense. The couple's emotional investment has been directed toward each other for many years, and a common bond grows out of shared experiences and achievements. The desire for closeness and emotional security tends to increase with age. It is precisely in old age, however, that this closeness can also be full of conflict. Every couple must seek to strike the right balance of togetherness and individuality, of closeness and distance, while mutually acknowledging their equality. Marital satisfaction depends significantly on the mutual willingness and ability to grow in this way because both needs and circumstances change in the course of individual development. The decisive factor is the ability to accept the unavoidable ups and downs of a life lived together without becoming resigned. When partners do not give up, they have the chance to find happiness again and again in their relationship.

SUMMARY

Many factors may have influenced the results of this study, which, unlike many others, utilized a nonclinical population of subjects. Responses were obtained through self-administered questionnaires sent through the mail and so may be different than if they had been administered in person by an interviewer. Other variations may be attributable to the fact that in seven countries respondents were married couples rather than couples living together, and couples with more than twenty-five years of marriage rather than those with more than twenty years of marriage. The Swedish study was the exception on these two criteria. The couples were mostly from urban areas, had a high socioeconomic status, and belonged to the same religion (mostly Catholics, Jews, and Protestants, depending on the country, with a sprinkling of Moslems and Hindus). Furthermore, the samples were relatively small. All these factors may alter the results when comparing the samples, making the generalizability from these findings somewhat limited.

In the majority of the countries involved, the DAS was used for the first time. The different variables correlated positively and had satisfactory reliability when calculated on Cronbach's alpha. The results of the study also indicate that the DAS seems to have reasonable validity. The results of the DAS from the different countries are very similar. The ingredients that couples consider most important for their satisfaction highlight love, fidelity, respect, mutual trust, and mutual support.

When considering the elements that motivate couples to stay together, there is also evidence of great similarity among respondents in all of the countries. Top priority is accorded to the conviction that crisis is inevitable and that marriage is a partnership for life. With these two characteristics emerging as so important, the authors urge that these two areas be emphasized in educational programs for youngsters before marriage or among newlyweds, who sometimes idealize marriage and deny the possibility of crisis. No marriage system is happy throughout its entire existence: Raising children, illnesses and accidents, loss of family members, and other normative and nonnormative changes in the family's life cycle require considerable adjustments by each member of the family, as well as by the couple as a team.

The fact that in some samples men reported higher satisfaction levels than women may occur because men have lower sensitivity to relationship disturbances than women. Nevertheless, no significant differences were found in the overall satisfaction between women and men. Significant differences were found only when comparing the very satisfied groups with the most dissatisfied group. King (1993) showed that emotional expressiveness is positively correlated with marital satisfaction. Kaslow and Hammerschmidt (1992) suggest that emotional stability that emanates from a consistently loving environment is the best predictor for the ability to commit to a long-term, intimate relationship. This statement is reinforced in the identification of the most significant variable, closeness, as the best predictor of a good-quality couple relationship. The majority of the couples in this study declared that they had happy childhoods and good relationships with their own parents before marriage.

Considering the samples from the eight countries involved, we conclude that couples who have been together for more than twenty-five years share a cluster of characteristics. The results reconfirm the basic characteristics believed to account for satisfying and lasting marriages: similarity and congruence of background, including religion, education, lifestyle, and philosophy of life; living in the present and future rather than the past; and intrinsic motivation as the basis of marriage.

This study highlights the fact that many researchers from different countries, who often spend their time doing research on or treating dysfunctional aspects of the family, can join together to focus on the salutogenic aspects of marriage and the family. In times when divorce is commonplace, it seems a necessity for mental health professionals, who do believe that many couples have satisfying marriages, to bring this fact and the substantiating evidence to the forefront.

Chapter 8

Retrospective Analysis: Conclusions, Implications for Therapy, and Recommendations

The vast majority of the 849 couples who participated in this study were in long-term marriages of twenty-five to forty-five years duration. The one exception was the study population in Sweden, where couples together only twenty-plus years were included. Some were in cohabiting situations without formal legalization of the commitment, but the relationships purportedly approximated marriage in all other respects.

The study populations were drawn from eight countries located on five different continents: Africa (South Africa); Europe (Germany, Sweden, and the Netherlands); North America (Canada and the United States); South America (Chile); and Asia (Israel).

In terms of socioeconomic status, data analyses reveal that the population was drawn from all strata of the economic scale, with a preponderance from the well-educated middle and upper-middle levels. A curve of normal distribution emerged, with the poorest couples drawn from the Israeli cohort of recent Russian immigrants; the wealthiest participants were part of the original pilot study in the United States as well as part of the German and South African respondent groups. Thus, it appears that people at all rungs of the socioeconomic ladder can achieve closeness and satisfaction in long-term marital relationships. Wealth does not appear to be an essential ingredient.

The emerging profile of the characteristics of long-term satisfied couples is a multifaceted one. What is most compelling is that despite the diversity in countries of origin, current residence, religion, socioeconomic status, vocation, and educational level, the similarity in the factors to which respondents attribute their satisfaction is great.

165

They may have rank ordered the essential ingredients slightly differently, but the same ones appear repeatedly. In combining these ingredients, a portrait emerges representing the main variables that characterize satisfied couples who have remained in marriages between twenty and forty-five years, regardless of differences in ethnic, cultural, and national background or other demographic factors. We believe the findings to be relevant for similar populations residing in countries beyond the eight from which the study samples were drawn. However, the findings cannot be generalized beyond the data, for example, to black, Asian, or American Indian couples, since those comprising the study populations were almost all Caucasian.

Subjects indicated that they were members of all of the major religions in the world, with the overwhelming majority being Catholic, Protestant, or Jewish. There were a few Hindu and Moslem respondents. Thus, specific religion does not seem to be a significant variable. What does seem salient is that the overwhelming majority report that their religious belief system supports the importance of viewing marriage as a covenant which should last "until death do us part." This underscores what was reported in all of the eight samples: that each partner needs to have a *commitment* to both the *institution* and permanency of marriage, as well as to the specific *partner*. Most respondents linked the values derived from their religion to their ongoing belief in the importance of a permanent marriage, and used their belief system as a source of sustenance during times of stress and crisis.

The main factors that emerged across respondent groups are listed below, but are not ranked in any order of importance. Rather, they have been clustered according to various terms conveying similar factors. Ingredients that were rated highly are listed alphabetically by the first key word, and some amplification is provided.

- Adaptability and flexibility
- Appreciation
- Coherence—each partner has a good inner sense of coherence; experience of congruence between them
- Compromise—ability to enter into give and take
- Communication skills—open, considerate, solid
- Commitment to partner and to institution of marriage

- Consideration and sensitivity—reciprocal
- Dependability and reliability—can count on each other
- Dyadic co-orientation
- Empathy—mutual
- Equality—good balance of power; seek win-win resolution of difference; each partner contributes to marriage as fully as possible
- Fairness
- Fidelity and faithfulness in all areas
- Friends—close confidants and companions
- Fun—enjoy each other; play well together; allocate time for pleasure, recreation, vacations
- Goals in life—clear and with plan for fulfillment (reevaluated periodically)
- Honesty and integrity
- Intimacy and sense of belonging together (and in larger family and friendship systems)
- Love and affection for each other
- Love and concern for children and grandchildren
- Love and concern for each other's family of origin
- Patience
- Problem solving—good ability together; solid track record over time
- Resilience
- Respect—mutual (positive regard for each other)
- Self-disclosure
- Sense of humor
- Sense of responsibility to partner and children
- Sexuality—ongoing and mutually enjoyable
- Shared interests and activities
- Shared values and lifestyle preferences
- Soul mates
- Spaces in togetherness—respect for each other's privacy and some separate interests; good balance between individual needs and couple needs
- Trustworthy and trusting (in areas beyond fidelity, i.e., money, keeping confidences)
- Understanding

This list also encompasses those traits that respondents indicated they desired more of in their partners—with particular emphasis on patience and understanding. It is noteworthy that the overwhelming majority of subjects reported that their parents had been in long-term marriages which they perceived as satisfying, and that by and large they considered their relationships with their own parents to have been (and still to be) quite good. This seems to convey, once again, an important message to parents—that if they are happily married and if they create a healthy relationship system within the family so that their children perceive their growing-up years as happy, then there is a high probability that their children will be content in the future and will enter into durable, satisfying relationships (Lewis et al., 1976; Kaslow, 1981; Walsh, 1982). The intergenerational transmission process so eloquently described by Bowen (1988) can transmit models of positive, collaborative, mutually satisfying relationships, as well as destructive patterns of interaction.

In some instances, the male member of the couple reported a higher level of satisfaction in the relationship than did his female partner. Interestingly, in the early years of marriage women seem to report more satisfaction, relishing the home and family—building aspects of a partnership such as security, predictability, and sense of belonging—while some men report feeling more tied down than they had anticipated by having to be accountable to and (partially) responsible for a wife and children. This seems to shift in the later years of the marital life cycle when men come to cherish the sanctity and security of home and the marital relationship, while their wives may need more independence, autonomy, and freedom from cooking and household chores. Once the children are gone, many women seek new experiences, including rewarding careers, time to do what they wish, and more excitement within the relationship, encompassing deeper levels of emotional intimacy. Some may become bored and disgruntled with their husbands, who now have more time available and are physically present, but are emotionally detached and/or critical. Couples in the study who exhibited patterns such as this were likely to have remained together for financial reasons or because they do not believe in divorce, do not expect a high level of satisfaction, and prefer some relationship to being alone. In terms of categories utilized in this study, such couples fall within the small percentage of those who report being dissatisfied or moderately satisfied, yet have chosen to remain in the marriage, for better or for worse. These are comparable to the stable/neutral and stable/negative marriages noted in the work of Weishaus and Field (1988), which was discussed in Chapter 2.

Many of the characteristics found to be essential in this research are similar to those identified by others. For example, Fennell (1987) found faith in God and spiritual commitment to be an important variable, just as we found that for the majority of our couples, a religious affiliation and belief system derived from their religion was an important underpinning for their unwavering commitment to marriage. It seems important in this summation to highlight the importance that the study respondents placed on the expectation and perception of mutuality in the kinds of positive behavioral exchanges stressed by behavioral therapists (Jacobson and Margolin, 1979). This reciprocity and the knowledge that it exists no doubt enhances feelings of well-being and camaraderie. These couples value their couple identity *and* also are connected to their extended family systems, friends, colleagues, and the community at large. They are able to mobilize resources from a variety of sources when need be, providing a rich field from which to draw. They do not feel isolated and as though no one cares, which also enables them to be more resourceful. Once again, a sharp divergence is seen between satisfied couples and those who are dissatisfied and dysfunctional, as the latter often feel quite alienated and lacking in resources.

Lauer, Lauer, and Kerr (1990) are one of the few groups of researchers who have studied couples married even longer than those in this study; their 100 couple respondents fell in the forty-five to sixty-five-year duration range. Four of the variables that they found are identical to those we listed previously:

- Being married to partners they liked as people and enjoyed being with
- Commitment to the spouse and to marriage
- A sense of humor
- Consensus on various matters such as aims and goals in life, friends, and decision making

Wallerstein and Blakeslee's (1995) fifty-couple study, on which they reported in *The Good Marriage: How and Why Love Lasts*, identified four kinds of enduring marriages: romantic, rescue, companionate, and traditional. We did not glean evidence that any of the satisfied couples in our various study groups fell predominantly in the rescue category. Rather, they seem to be a combination of companionate, traditional, and romantic, with these components manifesting in different proportions at different times in the course of the marriage. It is possible that those dyads in which rescuing played a large part in the interaction pattern typified the couples who scored as not satisfied on the Dyadic Adjustment Scale. Here again, we can posit a high level of concurrence across studies.

It seems important to reiterate at this point that even if a couple has been married for twenty-five-plus years, it is not necessarily valid to assume that they each experience high marital satisfaction. The data analysis revealed that even within this group, a minority of couples reported low marital satisfaction. As Gottman's study (1994) indicated, couples who stay together can be divided into three groups: (1) *volatile*—those who argue sometimes yet remain passionately involved with each other; (2) *validating*—those who are compatible, supportive, and appreciative of each other; and (3) *avoidant*—those who live parallel but somewhat separate lives while sharing the same residence. It is hypothesized that the high-satisfaction couples in this study fall into the first two categories, and that the low-satisfaction couples tend to become increasingly avoidant but opt, for a variety of reasons, not to separate. Their reasons appear to include fear of loneliness, commitment to importance of the ideal of family, mutual dependency, religious beliefs, and financial considerations, as well as being accustomed to the negative interaction patterns, which are perhaps more tolerable than the unknown problems of being alone or in a new relationship.

IMPLICATIONS FOR MARITAL AND FAMILY THERAPY

The aggregate extensive and elaborate list of ingredients, characteristics, and traits reported by the study respondents as typifying their marriages comes together in a lively Technicolor portrait.

Assuredly, not all of the couples have the same belief and value systems or lifestyle preferences. However, intracouple values, interests, and goals are remarkably similar. Probably this was less so in the early years of their relationship, but developed over time through negotiation, compromise, and the expansion of each one's horizons to take in the interests and ideas of the other. For those who were never able to accomplish this merging of what was significant for each, while still retaining their individuality and some separate interests, the marriages that endured were physically intact but emotionally detached and not rated as satisfying.

We believe that the portrait emerging from this research is (a) broad enough and yet specific enough in terms of the motives that lead people to create solid, caring, congenial relationships in which they have faith in their ability to resolve problems and disagreements that inevitably arise, and (b) representative of a large spectrum of the essential ingredients that characterize dynamic, flexible, interesting relationships that couples choose to preserve and nourish. Further, we recommend that those engaged in couples therapy be knowledgeable about this portrait as a vision toward which they can guide troubled couples. Being aware of this composite might lead clinicians to choose the variables that they find most relevant for the couples they see in therapy and to provide them with a list. Then they might codetermine which ones they wish to work toward as goals and prioritize them. For example, by helping them to work out a process for solving problems instead of screaming, disparaging one another, refusing to discuss the issue, or other ineffective behaviors, therapists can not only contribute to changing their patients' communication style but also can lead them to hear each other better and to have more respect for each other's wishes, feelings, and intelligence in finding meaningful solutions.

Discussion of the importance of couples' fun time, and even conveying permission to have fun together, can enhance their lives as they begin to have a weekly "date" and perhaps take turns selecting and planning what they will do, thus reawakening dormant interests and hobbies or exploring new ones while avoiding disagreements over what to do. By adding this dimension to their lives, they share more playfulness, laughter, and novelty, and provide balance to the everyday tasks of running a home, raising children, and earning a living. Alternating going out alone and socializing together with other couples can further enrich and revitalize their life together. In a more serious vein, dealing with each one's desire to be able to trust the other in all domains of life and to count on each other's honesty and integrity can lead each to try to think and behave in ways that make him or her trustworthy and dependable. Combining this with considering what does not work, such as prolonged hostile silences, being a "couch potato" and spending many long evenings watching television, and/or lying and deception, can enable couples to assess what has not proven to be acceptable. Furthermore, the process can help them to identify what modifications each needs to make in his or her attitudes and behaviors in order to fashion the kind of marriage that they will find rich with love and affection, as well as fulfilling, gratifying, mutually enhancing, and worth treasuring. Given that generally the more satisfied couples are also physically healthy, patients should be encouraged to consider improving their health and well-being through proper nutrition, frequent exercise, relaxation or meditation, ample rest, and good medical care.

We believe that these findings and conclusions are relevant, cogent, and applicable, both multiculturally within a given country and cross-culturally among a variety of countries, given that they were derived from eight quite diverse countries, each of which comprise a variegated population. The universality of the desire and need for physical, emotional, and spiritual well-being is reflected in the ingredients specified as essential for satisfaction in a marriage— the major relationship in which these needs can be fulfilled. The feelings toward each other may be expressed in ways that are unique and/or idiosyncratic to the individuals, their respective families, and/or communities, but the commonalties of the desire to be loved, respected, appreciated and trusted, to feel secure, and to share one's innermost hopes and dreams with a close friend and intimate companion cut across all religious and ethnic groups and socioeconomic strata. This is part and parcel of our essential shared humanity.

Appendix A

Overall Assessment
of the Quality of Couple Life

COUPLE WELL-BEING—DAS, ITEM 18

"In general, how often do you think that things between you and your partner are going well?"

- "bad"   never, rarely, occasionally   -1
- "middle"   more often than not   0
- "good"   most of the time   0.5
- "very good"   all the time   1

COUPLE SATISFACTION—DAS, SUBSCALE

- "dissatisfaction"   rating < 35
- "middle range"   rating = 35-42
- "satisfaction"   rating > 42

COUPLE HAPPINESS—DAS, ITEM 31

The points in the following list represent different degrees of happiness in your relationship. The point, "happy," represents the degree of happiness of most relationships. Please circle the point that best describes the degree of happiness, all things considered, of your relationship.

- "unhappy"   extremely, fairly, or a little unhappy   -1
- "happy"   happy   0
- "very happy"   very happy, extremely happy   0.5
- "extremely"   extremely, perfect   1

Appendix B

International Family Research Group Long-Term Marriages Questionnaire

INSTRUCTIONS FOR USER

Enclosed herewith you will find a cover letter to be distributed with the questionnaires to your respondents. Each couple should be given two complete sets of all the questionnaires, along with a prestamped envelope. The following five questionnaires are included in the package.

Q1. General Information:
- A. Personal Data
- B. Relationship with parents before marriage
- C. History of parents' relationships
- D. History of your marital relationship

Q2. Dyadic Adjustment Scale (DAS)
& Problem Rating List (PRL) (includes 40 items)

Q3. A. Couple Problem Solving (CPS)
- B. Couple Communication (CC)
- C. Couple Relationship (CR)

Q4. Motives (45 items)

Q5. Ingredients (43 items)

The following are some specific instructions and clarifications:

1. On the left-hand side of all questionnaires there are numbers for the use of computer analysis. Please do not change these numbers when you translate to your own language. In this way we will be able to do international comparisons.

2. The boxes on the upper right-hand corner are for code identification purposes:

> Numbers 1 and 2 for country identification
> Numbers 3 and 4 for questionnaire identification
> Numbers 5, 6, and 7 for individual identification

Please remember to fill in all three digits for the coding; e.g., if your sample will include 250 couples, start with 001-250. Remember to give both the husband and the wife the same number. It is advisable to give all pages the same numbers, so that in case they are separated for any reason, they can be reassembled correctly.

3. Each questionnaire begins with No. 8. For example, in Q.1. A, the first item is Sex: (1) female (2) male. Then for coding No. 8 you indicate (1) for female or (2) for male. No. 9-10 relates to item #2, the age; e.g., age 75 should be coded: $\underline{7}\ \underline{5}$, etc.
9 10

4. At the end of Q.1. (after #49) we left open numbers for each individual country to add some questions which are important to their own study. There are additional personal data required, e.g., "country of birth" or "Have you had family therapy during your marriage?" For these items we left coding numbers 50-75.

5. For each questionnaire there are specific instructions that should be easy to follow.

6. If you do not have access to a computer or are not familiar with coding and analyzing the data, please contact us directly for further assistance. It is also possible for us to do the analysis on our computer and forward the results to you.

Sample Cover Letter to Be Distributed with Questionnaire

INTERNATIONAL FAMILY RESEARCH GROUP

Dear Potential Respondents:

This cross-cultural study is geared to couples married between 25 and 46 years. Our goal is to explore essential ingredients in long-term marriage. Part 1 of this project originated in the United States. We hope that the results will help guide therapists and laypeople in knowing which types of behavior and attitudes are conducive to long-term, satisfying relationships and which fundamental skills can prevent severe crises in marriage.

We would appreciate very much if you could support our project through your participation, and motivate friends to do the same. We can guarantee you absolute anonymity, since we do not ask your name, profession, or address. Your privacy is our greatest commitment.

We therefore request that you comply strictly with the following instructions:

1. This questionnaire contains 15 pages. *Please complete all.*
2. It is important to fill out the questionnaires in the given sequence.
3. Please complete the questionnaires on your own, separately, in a quiet environment, since we want to know your own personal opinion. There is no such thing as absolute objectivity and it is completely normal that husbands and wives see things differently.
4. We are almost certain that these questionnaires will give you a great deal to think about. You may, of course, discuss these ideas with your partner after the completion of the questionnaires. Many of the couples who participated in a prior study reported benefits from discussing their responses after filling out their own forms.
5. Please do not compare your answers with those of your partner. Spontaneous answers are being sought.
6. Please be honest with yourself and with the researchers when answering the questions; otherwise we cannot compile relevant and true information.
7. When you have finished, please enclose the forms in the stamped envelope provided and mail it immediately.

We thank you in advance for taking time from your busy schedule to respond to this study.

Sincerely,

Florence Kaslow, PhD   Helga Hammerschmidt, Dipl-Psych
(United States)   (Germany)
Project Director   Project Co-Director

Shlomo A. Sharlin, PhD
(Israel)

1   7

Q.1. GENERAL INFORMATION

A. *Personal Data*

1. Sex: (1) female___ (2) male___

2. Age___

3. Religion:
   (1) Protestant___   (2) Catholic___   (3) Jewish___
   (4) Moslem___   (5) Other___

4. (1) Observant___   (2) Nonobservant___

5. Schooling: Number of years in:
   (1) Grade school___   (2) High school___
   (3) College___   (4) Post graduate___
   (5) Other___   (6) Total number of years___

6. Do you work?
   (1) Yes, full-time___   (2) Yes, part-time___   (3) No___

7. Your economic status:
   (1) Excellent___   (2) Very good___   (3) Good___
   (4) Fairly good___   (5) Bad___   (6) Very bad___

8. How would you assess your physical health compared with others in your age group?
   (1) Very good___   (2) Good___   (3) Moderate___
   (4) Bad___   (5) Very bad___

9. How was your childhood on the whole (until age 10)?
   (1) Very happy___   (2) Fairly happy___
   (3) Rather unhappy___   (4) Very unhappy___

B. *Relationship with Parents Before Marriage*

1. How much closeness was there between:

   You and your mother: (M)   You and your father: (F)
   (1) Quite a bit___   (1) Quite a bit___
   (2) Moderate___   (2) Moderate___
   (3) Little___   (3) Little___
   (4) None___   (4) None___

2. How much conflict was there between:

You and your mother: (M)
(1) A lot___
(2) Moderate___
(3) Little___
(4) None___

You and your father: (F)
(1) A lot___
(2) Moderate___
(3) Little___
(4) None___

C. History of Parents' Relationship

1. Length of your parents' marriage:___

2. Your parents' current marital status:
   (1) Still married___
   (2) Ended in divorce___
   (3) Ended in death___

3. Please give your appraisal of your parents' marriage:
   (1) Very happy___   (2) Fairly happy___
   (3) Rather unhappy___   (4) Very unhappy___

D. History of Your Marital Relationship

1. How long had you known your mate at the time of your marriage?
   (1) ___ weeks
   (2) ___ months
   (3) ___ years

2. How long did you "keep company" with your mate or live together before marriage?
   (1) not at all   (2) ___ weeks
   (3) ___ months   (4) ___ years

3. How old were you at the time of your marriage?___

4. Did you get married under pressure?
   (1) Yes___   (2) No___

   If yes, indicate for which of the following reasons:
   (1) family___   (2) economic reasons___
   (3) pregnancy___   (4) escape from parental home___
   (5) other___

   5. Marital status:
      (1) First marriage____   (2) Second marriage____
      (3) 3 or more marriages____   (4) Separated____
      (5) Divorced____   (6) Widowed____

   6. Number of years married (current):____

   7. Number of years married (previously):____

   8. Number of children from your present marriage:____

   9. Number of children from your present marriage:____

  10. Ages of children:____

1   7

Q.2. DAS AND PRL

Most persons have disagreements in their relationships. Please indicate below the approximate extent of agreement or disagreement between you and your partner for each item on the following list. Please circle the appropriate number in each case—*one only*—to indicate the answer that best describes your interaction.

Always agree	Almost always agree	Occa-sionally disagree	Frequently disagree	Almost always disagree	Always disagree
1	2	3	4	5	6

1. Handling family finances   1   2   3   4   5   6

2. Matters of recreation   1   2   3   4   5   6

3. Religious matters   1   2   3   4   5   6

4. Demonstration of affection   1   2   3   4   5   6

5. Friends   1   2   3   4   5   6

6. Sex relations   1   2   3   4   5   6

7. Conventionality (proper behavior)   1   2   3   4   5   6

8. Philosophy of life   1   2   3   4   5   6

9. Ways of dealing with parents or in-laws   1   2   3   4   5   6

10. Aims, goals, and things believed important   1   2   3   4   5   6

11. Amount of time spent together   1   2   3   4   5   6

12. Making major decisions   1   2   3   4   5   6

13. Household tasks   1   2   3   4   5   6

14. Leisure time interests and activities   1   2   3   4   5   6

15. Career decisions   1   2   3   4   5   6

All the time	Most of the time	More often than not	Occa-sionally	Rarely	Never
1	2	3	4	5	6

16. How often do you discuss or have you considered divorce, separation, or terminating your relationship?   1 2 3 4 5 6

17. How often do you or your mate leave the house after a fight?   1 2 3 4 5 6

18. In general, how often do you think things between you and your spouse are going well?   1 2 3 4 5 6

19. Do you confide in your mate?   1 2 3 4 5 6

20. Do you ever regret that you married (or lived together)?   1 2 3 4 5 6

21. How often do you and your partner quarrel?   1 2 3 4 5 6

22. How often do you and your mate "get on each other's nerves"?   1 2 3 4 5 6

23. Do you kiss your mate:
    (1) Every day   (2) Almost every day   (3) Occasionally
    (4) Rarely   (5) Never

24. Do you and your mate engage in outside interests together?
    (1) All the time   (2) Most of the time
    (3) Some of the time   (4) Very seldom   (5) Never

How often would you say the following events occur between you and your mate?

Never	Less than once a month	Once or twice a month	Once or twice a week	Once a day	More often
1	2	3	4	5	6

25. Have stimulating exchange of ideas?   1 2 3 4 5 6

26. Laugh together   1 2 3 4 5 6

27. Calmly discuss something   1   2   3   4   5   6

28. Work together on a project   1   2   3   4   5   6

There are some things about which couples sometimes agree and sometimes disagree. Indicate if either item below caused differences of opinion or were problems in your relationship during the past few weeks. (Check either Yes or No.)

29. Being too tired for sex. (1) Yes___ (2) No___

30. Not showing love. (1) Yes___ (2) No___

31. The points on the following line represent different degrees of happiness in your relationship. The middle point, "happy," represents the degree of happiness of most relationships. Please circle the point which best describes the degree of happiness, all things considered, of your relationship.

1	2	3	4	5	6	7
Extremely unhappy	Fairly unhappy	A little unhappy	Happy	Very happy	Extremely happy	Perfect

32. Which of the following statements best describes how you feel about the future of your relationship? *(Choose one only)*

    (1) I want desperately for my relationship to succeed, and would go to almost any length to see that it does.

    (2) I want very much for my relationship to succeed, and will do all I can to see that it does.

    (3) I want very much for my relationship to succeed, and will do my fair share to see that it does.

    (4) It would be nice if my relationship succeeded, but I cannot do much more than I am doing now to help it succeed.

    (5) It would be nice if it succeeded, but I refuse to do any more than I am doing now to keep the relationship going.

    (6) My relationship can never succeed, and there is no more that I can do to keep the relationship going.

Please indicate the extent of agreement or disagreement between you and your partner for the following issues:

Always agree	Almost always agree	Occa-sionally disagree	Frequently disagree	Almost always disagree	Always disagree	Does not exist
1	2	3	4	5	6	0

33. Children   1   2   3   4   5   6   0

34. Extramarital affairs   1   2   3   4   5   6   0

35. Abuse of alcohol, drugs, tobacco, food   1   2   3   4   5   6   0

36. Temper of spouse   1   2   3   4   5   6   –

37. Attractiveness, personal appearance   1   2   3   4   5   6   –

38. Jealousy   1   2   3   4   5   6   –

39. Habits of spouse   1   2   3   4   5   6   –

40. Personal freedom and space   1   2   3   4   5   6   –

1   7

Q.3. COUPLE PROBLEM SOLVING (CPS), COUPLE COMMUNICATION (CC), AND COUPLE RELATIONSHIPS (CR)

A. CPS

When you are under stress as a couple, what do you do?

Almost never	Occasion-ally	Some-times	Often		Very often
1	2	3	4		5

1. We make decisions impulsively.	1	2	3	4	5
2. There is little cooperation between us.	1	2	3	4	5
3. We have trouble finding new ways of solving our problems.	1	2	3	4	5
4. One person's bad mood makes the other person feel down.	1	2	3	4	5
5. We become more isolated and independent.	1	2	3	4	5
6. We become more disorganized.	1	2	3	4	5
7. We become more rigid and controlling of each other.	1	2	3	4	5
8. We find it difficult to have privacy and think things over.	1	2	3	4	5
9. We stay out of each other's way.	1	2	3	4	5
10. We rely more on friends and relatives than each other for support.	1	2	3	4	5

B. CC

Please describe your communication with your partner:

Almost never	Occasion- ally	Some- times	Often	Very often
1	2	3	4	5

1. It is easy for me to express all my true feelings to my partner.   1   2   3   4   5

2. My partner often gives me the silent treatment when we are having a problem.   1   2   3   4   5

3. My partner sometimes makes comments that put me down.   1   2   3   4   5

4. Sometimes I am afraid to ask my partner for what I want.   1   2   3   4   5

5. I wish my partner were more willing to share his or her feelings with me.   1   2   3   4   5

6. Sometimes I have trouble believing what my partner tells me.   1   2   3   4   5

7. Often I do not tell my partner what I am feeling because she or he should already know   1   2   3   4   5

8. I am satisfied with the way my partner and I talk to each other.   1   2   3   4   5

9. My partner is a good listener.   1   2   3   4   5

10. I do not share negative feelings I have about my partner because I am afraid she or he will get angry.   1   2   3   4   5

C. CR

Please indicate how you typically operate as a couple:

Almost never	Occasion-ally	Some-times	Often		Very often
1	2	3	4		5

1. We ask each other for help.	1	2	3	4	5
2. We compromise when problems arise.	1	2	3	4	5
3. We approve of each other's friends.	1	2	3	4	5
4. We are creative in how we handle differences.	1	2	3	4	5
5. We like to do things with each other.	1	2	3	4	5
6. We share the leadership.	1	2	3	4	5
7. Jealousy is an issue in our relationship.	1	2	3	4	5
8. We change our way of handling tasks.	1	2	3	4	5
9. We like to spend free time together.	1	2	3	4	5
10. We try new ways of dealing with problems.	1	2	3	4	5
11. We feel close to each other.	1	2	3	4	5
12. We jointly make the decisions.	1	2	3	4	5
13. We share hobbies and interests together.	1	2	3	4	5
14. We find our relationship changes over time.	1	2	3	4	5
15. We can easily think of things to do together.	1	2	3	4	5
16. We shift household responsibilities.	1	2	3	4	5
17. We consult each other on our decisions.	1	2	3	4	5
18. One person tries to be the leader.	1	2	3	4	5
19. We believe togetherness is a top priority.	1	2	3	4	5
20. We are flexible in our lifestyle.	1	2	3	4	5

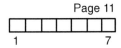
Q.4. MOTIVES:
WHY DID AND DO YOU STAY TOGETHER?

In the following list you find many reasons why couples decide to remain in their marriage.

Please mark three reasons in each category:

a.   Which are the most important to you NOW?

b.   Which were crucial during the most difficult stage of your marriage?

Now	Motives	Difficult Stage
	Because: 1. marriage is a partnership for life 2. I feel responsible to my partner 3. I feel responsible to our children 4. we have children 5. of my religious conviction 6. of pressure from church 7. of expectations of our family of origin 8. of pressure from our family of origin 9. of fear of negative impact on job or career 10. I enjoy our lifestyle and do not wish to change it 11. a splitting of our assets would destroy the economic basis of our existence 12. of financial dependence 13. I do not want to accept economic disadvantages 14. of the conviction that crises are inevitable 15. of the conviction that crises promote personal growth 16. of love 17. of good satisfying sexual relationship	

Now	Motives	Difficult Stage
	18. I believe I could not find a better partner in spite of a number of difficulties	
	19. we complement each other in spite of occasional tensions	
	20. I haven't yet found just cause for separation in spite of some difficulties	
	21. my partner has always behaved fairly even in crisis situations	
	22. we can shape our marital life ourselves	
	23. I can contribute something to shaping our marital life	
	24. we are prepared to accept the changes and challenges which make life exciting	
	25. one cannot give up easily on such crucial matters	
	26. our shared experiences have drawn us closely together	
	27. we appreciate our closeness and comfort with each other	
	28. I can adjust myself to my partner	
	29. we can adjust to one another	
	30. my partner is patient and understanding with me	
	31. we are patient and understanding with one another	
	32. I am convinced that we can resolve our problems	
	33. we have struck a good balance between independence and connectedness	
	34. I have learned to live with a less than satisfactory marriage	
	35. fate has brought us together	
	36. I still find my partner attractive	

Now	Motives	Difficult Stage
	37. I am admired for having this partner	
	38. I am afraid that my partner would not be able to cope by himself/herself	
	39. I am afraid that I would not be able to cope by myself	
	40. separation and divorce are considered a social stigma	
	41. I am afraid of change	
	42. my partner does not want to release me no matter what happens	
	43. our division of roles and responsibilities is practical	
	44. we have the ability to forgive	
	45. Other reasons:_____	
	_____	
	_____	
	_____	
	_____	
	_____	

1   7

Q.5. INGREDIENTS
FOR MARITAL SATISFACTION

Please indicate which ingredients:

a. exist presently in your marriage by making a check mark under category 1 (Q.5. A).

b. you would desire, by checking category 2 (Q.5. B).

You can choose a total of 10 items from both columns 1 and 2.

Ingredients	Categories	
	Q.5. A	Q.5. B
1. Mutual trust		
2. Mutual respect		
3. Mutual give and take		
4. Mutual support		
5. Shared interests		
6. Being patient and understanding		
7. Respect for each other's independence		
8. Openness, honesty, candor		
9. Frequent exchange of ideas		
10. Good problem-solving ability		
11. Similar philosophy of life		
12. Corresponding religious beliefs		
13. Cohesion		
14. Love		
15. Loyalty and fidelity		
16. Sensitivity and consideration for needs of spouse		
17. Sharing leisure time activities		
18. Mutual appreciation		
19. Expression of affection		
20. Consensus about sexual behavior		

	Categories	
Ingredients	Q.5. A	Q.5. B
21. Mutual sexual fulfillment	_____	_____
22. Happy atmosphere	_____	_____
23. Doing interesting things together	_____	_____
24. Permitting each other individual development	_____	_____
25. Making major decisions together	_____	_____
26. Reliability	_____	_____
27. Financial and general economic security	_____	_____
28. Clear role structure and responsibilities	_____	_____
29. Willingness to adjust and compromise	_____	_____
30. Complementarity	_____	_____
31. Shared interest in children	_____	_____
32. Avoiding repetition and boredom	_____	_____
33. Egalitarian relationship	_____	_____
34. Attractiveness of spouse	_____	_____
35. Fun and humor together	_____	_____
36. Mutual encouragement	_____	_____
37. Shared values	_____	_____
38. Balance between individuality and couplehood	_____	_____
39. Similar spiritual orientation	_____	_____
40. Feeling safe	_____	_____
41. Comradeship	_____	_____
42. Good listening	_____	_____
43. Other ingredients _____	_____	_____
_____	_____	_____
_____	_____	_____
_____	_____	_____
_____	_____	_____

References

Chapter 1

Ahrons, C.R. and Rogers, R.H. (1987). *Divorced families: A multidisciplinary developmental view.* New York: W.W. Norton.

Antonovsky, A. (1988). *Unraveling the mystery of health.* San Francisco: Jossey Bass.

Beavers, W.R. (1977). *Psychotherapy and growth: A family systems perspective.* New York: Brunner/Mazel.

Beavers, W.R. (1982). Healthy, midrange and severely dysfunctional families. In F. Walsh (Ed.), *Normal family processes* (pp. 45-66). New York: Guilford.

Bowen, M. (1976). Theory in the practice of psychotherapy. In P.J. Guerin (Ed.), *Family therapy: Theory and practice* (pp. 42-90). New York: Gardner Press.

Cohen, R. (1998). Long-term marriages in Canada. Unpublished paper.

Fennell, D.L. (1987). *Characteristics of long-term first marriages.* Paper presented at 45th Annual American Association for Marriage and Family Therapy Conference, Chicago.

Fields, N.S. (1983). *The well seasoned marriage.* New York: Gardner Press.

Fincham, F.D. (1991). Understanding close relationships: An attributional perspective. In S. Zelen (Ed.), *New models: New extension of attributional theory* (pp. 163-206). New York: Springer Verlag.

Finkelstein, L.J. (1996). Long-term satisfying marriages in Netherlands. Unpublished paper.

Gibran, K. (1923). *The prophet.* New York: Knopf (reprinted 1975).

Gottman, J.M. and Levenson, R.W. (1992). Marital processes predictive of later dissolution: Behavior, physiology, and health. *Journal of Personality and Social Psychology*, 63(2): 221-233.

Greeley, A. (1981). The state of the nation's happiness. *Psychology Today*, 15(1): 14-17.

Hammerschmidt, H. and Kaslow, F.W. (1995). Langzeitehen: Eine analyse der zufriedenheit. *Familiendynamik*, 20(1): 97-115.

Kaslow, F.W. (1981). Divorce and divorce therapy. In A. Gurman and D. Kniskern (Eds.), *Handbook of family therapy* (pp. 662-696). New York: Brunner/Mazel.

Kaslow, F.W. (1982). Portrait of a healthy couple. *Psychiatric Clinics of North America*, 5(3): 519-527.

Kaslow, F.W. (1994). Painful partings: Providing therapeutic guidance. In L.L. Schwartz (Ed.), *Mid-life divorce counseling* (pp. 67-82). Alexandria, VA: American Counseling Association.

Kaslow, F.W. (1995). Descendants of Holocaust victims and perpetrators: Legacies and dialogue. *Contemporary Family Therapy*, 17(3): 275-290.

Kaslow, F.W. (1997). A dialogue between descendants of perpetrators and victims. *Israel Journal of Psychiatry*, 34(1): 44-54.

Kaslow, F.W. and Hammerschmidt, H.L. (1992). Long-term "good" marriages: The seemingly essential ingredients. *Journal of Couples Therapy*, 3(2/3): 15-38.

Kaslow, F.W., Hansson, K., and Lundblad, A.M. (1994). Long-term marriages in Sweden: And some comparisons with similar couples in the United States. *Contemporary Family Therapy*, 16(6): 521-537.

Kaslow, F.W. and Robison, J.A. (1996). Long-term satisfying marriages: Perceptions of contributing factors. *American Journal of Family Therapy*, 24(2): 153-170.

Lewis, J., Beavers, W.R., Gosset, J.T., and Phillips, V.A. (1976). *No single thread: Psychological health in family systems.* New York: Brunner/Mazel.

Meyerowitz, J.B. (1996). *Long-term satisfying marriages in South Africa.* Unpublished paper.

Murstein, B. (1980). Mate selection in the 1970s. *Journal of Marriage and the Family*, 42(4): 777-792.

Roizblatt, A., Kaslow, F.W., Rivera, S., Fuchs, T., Conejero, C., and Zacharias, A. (1999). Long-lasting marriages in Chile. *Contemporary Family Therapy*, 21(1): 113-129.

Schlesinger, B. (1982). Lasting marriages in the 1890s. *Conciliation Courts Review*, 16(2): 111-117.

Schlesinger, B. and Schlesinger, R. (1987). Lasting marriages and families: Accentuating the positive. *Sciences Pastorales*, 6(1): 25-37.

Schwartz, L.L. and Kaslow, F.W. (1997). *Painful partings: Divorce and its aftermath.* New York: John Wiley & Sons.

Sharlin, S.A. (1996). Long-term successful marriages in Israel. *Contemporary Family Therapy*, 18(2): 225-242.

Spanier, G.B. (1976). Measuring dyadic adjustment: New scales for assessing the quality of marriage and similar dyads. *Journal of Marriage and the Family*, 38(1): 15-28.

Wallerstein, J.S. and Blakeslee, S. (1995). *The good marriage: How and why love lasts.* New York: Houghton Mifflin Co.

Walsh, F. (Ed.) (1982). *Normal family process.* New York: Guilford.

Willi, J. (1991). *Was hält Paare zusammen?* Reinbek, Germany: Rowohlt.

Chapter 2

Antonovsky, A. (1988). *Unraveling the mystery of health.* San Francisco: Jossey Bass.

Antonovsky, A. (1992, February). Salutogenesis. *The Sense of Coherence Newsletter*, No. 4.

Bandura, A. (1977). *Social learning theory.* Englewood Cliffs, NJ: Prentice-Hall.

Barnes, H., Schumm, W., Jurich, A., and Bolman, S. (1984). Marital satisfaction: Positive regard versus effective communication as explanatory variables. *The Journal of Social Psychology*, 123(1): 71-78.

Beavers, W.R. (1985). *Successful marriage*. New York: Norton.

Bloom, B.L. and Hodges, W.W. (1981). The predicament of newly separated. *Community Mental Health Journal*, 17(4): 277-293.

Bowen, M. (1988). *Family therapy in clinical practice*. New York: Aronson.

Brandstädter, J., Baltes-Goetz, B., and Heil, F. (1990). Entwicklung in Partnerschaften: Analysen zur Partnerschaftsqualität bei Ehepaaren im mittleren Erwachsenenalter. *Zeitschrift für Entwicklungspsychologie und Paedagogische Psychologie*, 22 (3): 183-206.

Burr, W.R. (1970). Satisfaction with various aspects of marriage over the life cycle: A random middle class sample. *Journal of Marriage and the Family*, 32(1): 29-37.

Fennell, D.L. (1987). *Characteristics of long-term first marriages*. Paper presented at 45th annual American Association for Marriage and Family Therapy Conference, Chicago.

Glenn, N. (1990). Quantitative research on marital quality in the 1980s: A critical review. *Journal of Marriage and the Family*, 52(3): 818-831.

Gottman, J.M. (1994). *Why marriages succeed or fail*. New York: Simon and Schuster.

Gottman, J.M. and Krokoff, L.J. (1989). Marital interaction and satisfaction: A longitudinal view. *Journal of Consulting and Clinical Psychology*, 57(1): 47-62.

Gottman, J.M., Notarius, C., Gonso, J., and Markman, H. (1976). *A couple's guide to communication*. Champaign, IL: Research Press.

Hahlweg, K. and Markman, H.J. (1988). The effectiveness of behavioral marital therapy: Empirical status of behavioral techniques in preventing and alleviating marital distress. *Journal of Consulting and Clinical Psychology*, 56(3): 440-447.

Hahlweg, K., Revenstorf, D., and Schindler, L. (1984). Effects of behavioral marital therapy on couples' communication and problem-solving skills. *Journal of Consulting and Clinical Psychology*, 52(4): 533-566.

Hammerschmidt, H.L. and Kaslow, F.W. (1995). Langzeitehen: Eine Analyse der Zufriedenheit. *Familiendynamik*, 20(1): 97-115.

Hansen, J. and Schuldt, W. (1984). Marital self-disclosure and marital satisfaction. *Journal of Marriage and the Family*, 46(4): 923-926.

Hendrick, S. (1981). Self-disclosure and marital satisfaction. *Journal of Personality and Social Psychology*, 40(6): 1150-1159.

Huston, T.L. and Levinger, G. (1978). Interpersonal attraction and relationships. *Annual Review of Psychology*, 29: 115-156.

Jacobson, M.P. and Margolin, G. (1979). A stimulus control model for change in behavioral marital therapy: Implications for contingency contracting. *Journal of Marriage and Family Counseling*, 4(1): 29-35.

Kaslow, F.W. (1982). Portrait of a healthy couple. *Psychiatric Clinics of North America*, 5(3): 519-527.

Kaslow, F.W. and Hammerschmidt, H.L. (1992). Long term "good" marriages: The seemingly essential ingredients. *Journal of Couples Therapy*, 3(2/3): 15-38.

Kaslow, F., Hansson, K., and Lundblad, A.M. (1994). Long term marriages in Sweden: And some comparisons with similar couples in the United States. *Contemporary Family Therapy*, 16(6): 521-537.

Kayser, K. (1993). *When love dies: The process of marital disaffection.* New York: Guilford.

Kelley, H. (1983). Love and commitment. In H. Kelley, E. Berscheild, A. Christensen, J. Harvey, T. Huston, G. Levinger, E. McClintock, L.A. Peplau, and D.R. Peterson (Eds.), *Close relationships* (pp. 265-314). New York: Freeman.

Kerckhoff, A.C. and Davis, K.E. (1962). Value consensus and need complementarity in mate selection. *American Sociological Review*, 27(3): 295-303.

Lauer, R., Lauer, J., and Kerr, S. (1990). The long-term marriage: Perceptions of stability and satisfaction. *International Journal of Aging and Human Development*, 31(3): 189-195.

Levenson, R.W. and Gottman, J.M. (1983). Marital interaction: Physiological linkage and affective exchange. *Journal of Personality and Social Psychology*, 45(3): 587-597.

Lewis, R.A. and Spanier, G.B. (1979). Theorizing about the quality and stability of marriage. In W.R. Burr, R. Hill, F.I. Nye, and I.L. Reiss (Eds.), *Contemporary theories about the family*, Vol. 1 (pp. 268-294). New York: The Free Press.

Luckey, E.B. and Bain, J.K. (1970). Children: A factor in marital satisfaction. *Journal of Marriage and the Family*, 32(1): 43-44.

Margolin, G. and Wampold, B.E. (1981). Sequential analysis of conflict and accord in distressed and nondistressed marital partners. *Journal of Clinical and Consulting Psychology*, 49(4): 554-567.

Markman, H.J. and Hahlweg, K. (1993). The prediction and prevention of marital distress: An international perspective. *Clinical Psychology Review*, 13(1): 29-43.

Markman, H.J., Stanley, S., Floyd, F., and Blumberg, S. (1991). The Premarital Relationship Enhancement Program (PREP): Current status. *International Programs of Psychotherapy Research*, American Association-Society for Psychotherapy Research.

McCubbin, H.I. and Patterson, J.M. (1983). The family stress process: The double ABCX model of adjustment and social stress and the family: Adaptation. In H.I. McCubbin, M.B. Sussmann, and J.M. Patterson (Eds.), *Advances and developments in family stress theory and research* (pp. 7-37). Binghamton, NY: The Haworth Press, Inc.

Murstein, B.I. (1970). Stimulus—value—role: A theory of marital choice. *Journal of Marriage and the Family*, 32(3): 465-481.

Murstein, B. (1980). Mate selection in the 1970's. *Journal of Marriage and the Family*, 42(4): 777-792.

Notarius, C. and Markman, H. (1993). *We can work it out—Making sense of marital conflict.* New York: Putnam's Sons.

Notarius, C. and Vancetti, N.A. (1983). The marital agendas protocol. In E.E. Filsinger (Ed.), *Marriage and family assessment* (pp. 209-227). Beverly Hills, CA: Sage.

Olson, D. (1988). Family types, family stress and family satisfaction: A developmental perspective. In C. Falicov (Ed.), *Family transitions* (pp. 55-79). New York: Guilford.

Olson, D. (1996). Family stress and coping: A multi-system perspective. In M. Cusinato (Ed.), *Research on family resources and needs across the world* (pp. 73-106). Milano: LED.

Olson, D.H. and Stewart, K.L. (1990). *Multisystem assessment of health and stress (MASH MODEL).* Unpublished manuscript.

Olson, D.H. and Stewart, K.L. (1991). Family systems and health behaviors. In H.E. Schroeder (Ed.), *New directions in health psychology assessment* (pp. 27-64). New York: Hemisphere Publishing Corp.

Revenstorf, D., Hahlweg, K., Schindler, L., and Vogel, B. (1985). Interaction analysis of marital conflict. In K. Hahlweg and N. Jacobsen (Eds.), *Marital interaction: Analysis and modification* (pp. 121-183). New York: Guilford Press.

Rollins, B.C. and Cannon, K.L. (1974). Marital satisfaction over the family life cycle: A reevaluation. *Journal of Marriage and the Family,* 36(2): 271-282.

Rollins, B.C. and Feldman, H. (1970). Marital satisfaction over the family life cycle. *Journal of Marriage and the Family,* 32(1): 20-28.

Schwarzenhauer, W. (1980). Was macht eine Ehe gluecklich? *Partnerberatung,* 2(1): 49-65.

Sharlin, S.A. (1996). Long-term successful marriages in Israel. *Contemporary Family Therapy,* 18 (2): 225-242.

Spanier, G.B. (1976). Measuring dyadic adjustment: New scales for assessing the quality of marriage and similar dyads. *Journal of Marriage and the Family,* 47(1): 15-28.

Storaasli, R.D. and Markman, H.J. (1990). Relationship problems in the premarital and early stages of marriage: A test of family development theory. *Journal of Family Psychology,* 4(1): 80-98.

Terman, L.M., Buttenweiser, P., Ferguson, R.W., Johnson, W.B., and Wilson, D.P. (1938). *Psychological factors in marital happiness.* New York: McGraw Hill.

Ting-Toomey, S. (1982). An analysis of verbal communication patterns in high and low marital adjustment groups. *Human Communications Research,* 9(3): 291-302.

Wallerstein, J.S. and Blakeslee, S. (1995). *The good marriage: How and why love lasts.* New York: Houghton Mifflin.

Weishaus, S. and Field, D. (1988). A half century of marriage: Continuity or change? *Journal of Marriage and the Family,* 50: 763-774.

Welter-Enderlin, R. (1992). *Paare: Leidenschaft und lange Weile.* Zürich: Serie Piper.

Willi, J. (1975/1990). *Die Zweierbeziehung* (Couples in collusion). Reinbek, Germany: Rowohlt.

Willi, J. (1991). *Was hält Paare zusammen?* Reinbek, Germany: Rowohlt.

Winch, R.F. (1958). *Mate selection: A study of complementary needs.* New York: Harper & Brothers.

Chapter 3

Antonovsky, A. (1988). *Unraveling the mystery of health.* San Francisco: Jossey Bass.

Antonovsky, A. (1992, February). Salutogenesis. *The Sense of Coherence Newsletter,* No. 4.

Crane, D.R., Busby, D.M., and Larson, J.H. (1991). A factor analysis of the dyadic adjustment scale with distressed and nondistressed couples. *American Journal of Family Therapy,* 19(1): 60-66.

Hahlweg, K., Hank, G., and Klam, N. (1990). *Diagnostische Verfahren für Berater: Deutsche Version der Dyadic Adjustment Scale.* Weinheim: Beltz-Test.

Hammerschmidt, H.L. and Kaslow, F.W. (1995). Langzeitehen: Eine Analyse der Zufriedenheit. *Familiendynamik,* 20(1): 97-115.

Kaslow, F. and Hammerschmidt, H.L. (1992). Long-term "good" marriages: The seemingly essential ingredients. *Journal of Couples Therapy,* 3(2/3): 15-38.

Kuzel, A.J. (1992). Sampling in qualitative inquiry. In B.F. Crabtree and W.L. Miller (Eds.), *Doing qualitative research* (pp. 31-44). Newbury Park, CA: Sage.

Lewis, R.A. and Spanier, G.B. (1979). Marital quality, marital stability and social exchange. In F.I. Nye (Ed.), *Family relationship: Rewards and costs* (pp. 49-65). Beverly Hills, CA: Sage.

Locke, H.J. and Wallace, K.M. (1959). Short marital adjustment and prediction tests: Their reliability and validity. *Marriage and Family Living,* 21: 251-255.

Olson, D.H. and Stewart, K.L. (1991). Family systems and health behaviors. In H.E. Schroeder (Ed.), *New directions in health psychology assessment* (pp. 27-64). New York: Hemisphere Publishing Corp.

Sabatelli, R.M. (1988). Measurement issues in marital research: A review and critique of contemporary survey instruments. *Journal of Marriage and the Family,* 50(4): 891-915.

Schneewind, K., Weiss, J., and Olson, D. (1992). *Coping and stress profile: German analysis.* Unpublished paper.

Sharpley, C. and Cross, D. (1982). A psychometric evaluation of the Spanier dyadic adjustment scale. *Journal of Marriage and the Family,* 44(3): 739-741.

Spanier, G.B. (1976). Measuring dyadic adjustment: New scales for assessing the quality of marriages and similar dyads. *Journal of Marriage and the Family,* 38(1): 15-28.

Spanier, G. and Thompson, L. (1982). A confirmatory analysis of the dyadic adjustment scale. *Journal of Marriage and the Family,* 44(3): 731-738.

Thompson, L. and Spanier, G. (1983). The end of marriage and acceptance of marital termination. *Journal of Marriage and the Family,* 45(1): 103-113.

Chapter 4

Antonovsky, A. (1988). *Unraveling the mystery of health.* San Francisco: Jossey Bass.

Antonovsky, A. (1992, February). Salutogenesis. *The Sense of Coherence Newsletter,* No. 4.

Antonovsky, A. (1993). The structure and properties of the sense of coherence scale. *Social Science and Medicine,* 36(6): 725-733.

Barth, J. (1993). *It runs in my family: Overcoming the legacy of family illness.* New York: Brunner/Mazel.

Beavers, W.R. (1982). Healthy, mid-range and severely dysfunctional families. In F. Walsh (Ed.), *Normal family process* (pp. 45-66). New York: Guilford Press.

Beavers, W.R. (1985). *Successful marriage.* New York: W.W. Norton.

Bowen, M. (1988). *Family therapy in clinical practice.* New York: Jason Aronson.

Buber, M. (1937). *I and Thou.* Edinburgh: T & T Clark.

Burgess, E.W. and Wallin, P. (1953). *Engagement in marriage.* Philadelphia: Lippincott.

Dahlin, L. and Cederblad, M. (1993). Salutogenesis. Protective factors for individuals brought up in high risk environment with regard to the risk of psychiatric or social disorder. *Nordic Journal of Psychiatry,* 47(1): 53-60.

Duffy, A. (1988). Struggling with power: Feminist critiques of family inequality. In N. Mandell and A. Duffy (Eds.), *Restructuring the Canadian family: Feminist perspectives.* Toronto: Butterworths Canada Ltd.

Fennell, D.L. (1987). *Characteristics of long-term first marriages.* Paper presented at forty-fifth Annual American Association for Marriage & Family Therapy Conference, Chicago.

Gottman, J.M. (1994). *What predicts divorce? The relationship between marital processes and marital outcomes.* Hillsdale, NJ: Lawrence Erlbaum.

Gottman, J.M. and Krokoff, L.J. (1989). Marital interaction and satisfaction: A longitudinal view. *Journal of Consulting and Clinical Psychology,* 57(1): 47-52.

Healthy families featured in Washington conference. (1990, July/August). *Family Therapy News,* p. 8.

Johnson, M.P. (1982). Social and cognitive features of the dissolution of commitment to relationships. In S. Duck (Ed.), *Personal relationships 4: Dissolving personal relationships* (pp. 51-73). London: Academic Press.

Kaslow, F.W. (1993). Attractions and affairs: Fabulous and fatal. *Journal of Family Psychotherapy,* 4(4): 1-34.

Kaslow, F.W. and Hammerschmidt, H.L. (1992). Long-term "good" marriages: The seemingly essential ingredients. *Journal of Couples Therapy,* 3(2/3): 15-38.

Kaslow, F.W., Hansson, K., and Lundblad, A.M. (1994). Long-term marriages in Sweden: And some comparisons with similar couples in the United States. *Contemporary Family Therapy* 16(6): 521-537.

Kaslow, F.W. and Robison, J.A. (1996). Long term satisfying marriages: Perception of contributing factors. *American Journal of Family Therapy*, 24(2): 153-170.

Kaslow, F.W. and Schwartz, L.L. (1987). *Dynamics of divorce: A life cycle perspective.* New York: Brunner/Mazel.

Lewis, J., Beavers, W.R., Gossett, J.T., and Phillips, V.A. (1976). *No single thread: Psychological health in family systems.* New York: Brunner/Mazel.

Maslow, A. (1970). *Motivation and personality.* New York: Van Nostrand.

Meyerowitz, J.B. (1996). *Long-term satisfying marriages in South Africa.* Unpublished paper.

Miller, B.C. and Olson, D.H.L. (1976). *Cluster analysis as a method for defining types of marriage interaction.* Paper presented at National Council on Family Relations, Chicago.

Murstein, B. (1980). Mate selection in the 1970s. *Journal of Marriage and the Family*, 42(4): 777-792.

Nawran, L. (1967). Communication and adjustment in marriage. *Family Process*, 6(2): 173-184.

Rollins, B.C. and Cannon, K.L. (1974). Marital satisfaction over the family life cycle: A reevaluation. *Journal of Marriage and the Family*, 36(2): 271-282.

Schwarzenhauer, W. (1980). Was macht eine Ehe glueclich? *Partnerberatung*, 2(1): 49-65.

Sharlin, S.A. (1996). Long-term successful marriages in Israel. *Contemporary Family Therapy*, 18(2): 225-242.

Spanier, G.B. (1976). Measuring dyadic adjustment: New scales for assessing the quality of marriage and similar dyads. *Journal of Marriage and the Family*, 38(1): 15-28.

Spanier, G.B. (1989). *Manual for the dyadic adjustment scale.* North Tonawanda, NY: Multi-Health Systems.

Stuart, R.B. (1980). *Helping couples change: A social learning approach to marital therapy.* New York: Guilford Press.

Swensen, C. and Trahaug, G. (1985). Commitment and the long-term marriage relationship. *Journal of Marriage and the Family*, 47(4): 939-945.

Willette-Bloom, M.C. and Nock, S.L. (1992). The effects of childhood family structure and perception of parents' marital happiness on familial aspirations. *Journal of Divorce and Remarriage*, 18(3-4): 3-23.

Willi, J. (1975/1990). *Die Zweierbeziehung.* (Couples in collusion.) Reinbek, Germany: Rowohlt.

Wynne, L., Ryckoff, I., Day, J., and Hirsh, S.H. (1958). Pseudo-mutuality in schizophrenia. *Psychiatry*, 21(2): 205-220.

Chapter 5

Antonovsky, A. (1988). *Unraveling the mystery of health.* San Francisco: Jossey Bass.

Antonovsky, A. (1992, February). Salutogenesis. *The Sense of Coherence Newsletter*, No. 4.

Brandstädter, J., Baltes-Goetz, B., and Heil, F. (1990). Entwicklung in Partnerschaften: Analysen zur Partnerschaftsqualität bei Ehepaaren im mittleren Erwachsenenalter. *Zeitschrift für Entwicklungspsychologie und Paedagogische Psychologie*, 22(3): 183-206.

Byrne, D. and Murnen, S. (1988). Maintaining loving relationships. In R. Sternberg and M. Barnes (Eds.), *The psychology of love* (pp. 293-310). New Haven, CT: Yale University Press.

Dahlin, L. and Cederblad, M. (1993). Salutogenesis. Protective factors for individuals brought up in high-risk environment with regard to the risk for a psychiatric or social disorder. *Nordic Journal of Psychiatry*, 47(1): 53-60.

Furhoff, A.M. and Olsson, L. (1993). Aktenskapet—parforhallandet. Hur blir relationen bra och veraktig. Forskning och utveckling, Landstinget Skaraborg. Unpublished paper.

Gottman, J.M. (1994). *What predicts divorce? The relationship between marital processes and marital outcomes*. Hillsdale, NJ: Lawrence Erlbaum.

Gottman, J.M. and Krokoff, L.J. (1989). Marital interaction and satisfaction: A longitudinal view. *Journal of Consulting and Clinical Psychology*, 57(1): 47-62.

Hahlweg, K., Hank, G., and Klam, N. (1990). *Diagnostische Verfahren für Berater: Deutsche Version der Dyadic Adjustment Scale*. Weinheim: Beltz-Test.

Hammerschmidt, H.L. and Kaslow, F. (1995). Langzeitehen: Eine Analyse der Zufriedenheit. *Familiendynamik*, 20(1): 97-115.

Hansson, K.M., Lundblad, A.M., and Kaslow, F.W. (1994). Langa aktenskap (Long-term marriages). *Nordisk Psyuchologi*, 2(3): 35-47.

Harper, J.M. and Elliott, M.L. (1988). Can there be too much of a good thing? The relationship between desired level of intimacy and marital adjustment. *The American Journal of Family Therapy*, 16(4): 351-360.

Hazan, C. and Shaver, P. (1987). Romantic love conceptualized as an attachment process. *Journal of Personality and Social Psychology*, 52(3): 511-524.

Hunter, J. and Schmidt, F. (1990). *Methods of meta analysis*. Newbury Park, CA: Sage Publications.

Kaslow, F.W. and Hammerschmidt, H.L. (1992). Long-term "good" marriages: The seemingly essential ingredients. *Journal of Couples Therapy*, 3(2/3): 15-38.

Kaslow, F.W., Hansson, K., and Lundblad, A.M. (1994). Long-term marriages in Sweden and some comparisons with similar couples in the United States. *Contemporary Family Therapy*, 16(6): 521-537.

Kuzel, A.J. (1992). Sampling in qualitative inquiry. In B.F. Crabtree and W.L. Miller (Eds.), *Doing qualitative research* (pp. 31-44). Newbury Park, CA: Sage.

Lenneer-Axelsson, B. (1989). *Mannens roster*. Stockholm: Sesam.

Lewis, R.A. and Spanier, G.B. (1979). Theorizing about the quality and stability of marriage. In W.R. Burr, R. Hill, F.I. Nye, and I.L. Reis (Eds.), *Contemporary theories about the family*, Vol. 1 (pp. 268-294). New York: The Free Press.

Minuchin, S. (1974). *Families and family therapy.* Cambridge, MA: Harvard University Press.

Olson, D. (1988). Family types, family stress and family satisfaction: A developmental perspective. In C. Falicov (Ed.), *Family transitions* (pp. 55-79). New York: Guilford.

Olson, D.H. and Stewart, K.L. (1991). Family systems and health behaviors. In H.E. Schroeder (Ed.), *New directions in health psychology assessment* (pp. 27-64). New York: Hemisphere Publishing Corp.

Spanier, G. (1976). Measuring dyadic adjustment: New scales for assessing the quality of marriage and similar dyads. *Journal of Marriage and the Family,* 47(1): 15-28.

Statistish Arsbok (1993). (Statistics Yearbook)—Stockholm: Statistics Sweden. Publication Serveces.

Walsh, F. (Ed.) (1982). *Normal family processes.* New York: Guilford.

Weitzman, L.J. (1985). *The divorce revolution: The unexpected social and economic consequences for women and children in America.* New York: Free Press.

Willi, J. (1975/1990). *Die Zweierbeziehung* (The dyadic relationship). Reinbek bei Hamburg: Rowohlt Taschenbuchverlag GmbH.

Willi, J. (1985/1989). *Ko-evolution, die Kunst des gemeinsamen Wachsens* (Co-evolution, the art of growing together). Reinbek, Germany: Rowohlt.

Chapter 6

Bowen, M. (1976). Theory in the practice of psychotherapy. In P.J. Guerin Jr. (Ed.), *Family therapy, theory and practice* (pp. 42-90). New York: Gardner Press.

de Waal, M. (1990). *Die Verintensis Van Blanke Geroude Persone Tot Die Huwelik* (White married couples' commitment to marriage). Johannesburg: Randse Afrikaanse Universiteit.

Erikson, E.H. (1965). *Childhood and society.* Harmondsworth, U.K.: Penguin.

Fennell, D.L. (1987). *Characteristics of long-term first marriages.* Paper presented at 45th Annual American Association for Marriage and Family Therapy Conference, Chicago.

Kaslow, F.W. and Hammerschmidt, H.L. (1992). Long-term "good" marriages: The seemingly essential ingredients. *Journal of Couples Therapy,* 3(2/3): 15-38.

Kaslow, F.W. and Robison, J.A. (1996). Long-term satisfying marriages: Perceptions of contributing factors. *American Journal of Family Therapy,* 24(2): 153-170.

Roizblatt, A., Fuchs, T., and Rivera, S. (1966). *Long lasting marriages in Chile.* Santiago: Universidad de Chile.

Roizblatt, A., Kaslow, F.W., Rivera, S., Fuchs, T., Conejero, C., and Zacharias, A. (1999). Long lasting marriages in Chile. *Contemporary Family Therapy,* 21(1): 113-129.

Sharlin, S.A. (1996). Long-term successful marriages in Israel. *Contemporary Family Therapy,* 18(2): 225-242.

South African Central Statistical Survey. (1995). *Statistical Abstract. 1995.* Johannesburg: Author.

Spanier, G.B. (1976). Measuring dyadic adjustment: New scales for assessing the quality of marriage and similar dyads. *Journal of Marriage and the Family,* 38(1): 15-28.

Spanier, G.B. (1988). Assessing the strengths of the Dyadic Adjustment Scale. *Journal of Marriage and the Family,* 44(3): 92-94.

Wallerstein, J.S. and Blakeslee, S. (1995). *The good marriage: How and why love lasts.* New York: Houghton Mifflin Co.

Willi, J. (1993). *Was hält Paare zusammen?* Reinbek, Germany: Rowohlt.

Willi, J. (1994). *Die Zweierbeziehung* (The dyadic relationship). Reinbek bei Hamburg: Rowohlt Taschenbuchverlag GmbH.

Chapter 7

Branden, N. (1988). A vision of romantic love. In R.J. Sternberg and M.L. Barnes (Eds.), *Psychology of love* (pp. 218–231). New Haven, CT: Yale University Press.

Central Bureau of Statistics, Israel. (1996). *Statistical abstract of Israel,* Vol. 77. Jerusalem: Hemed Press.

Kaslow, F.W. and Hammerschmidt, H.L. (1992). Long-term "good" marriages: The seemingly essential ingredients. *Journal of Couples Therapy,* 3(2/3): 15-38.

Kurian, G.T. (Ed.) (1991). *The new book of world rankings.* New York: Facts on File.

King, L.A. (1993). Emotional expression, ambivalence over expression, and marital satisfaction. *Journal of Social and Personal Relationshpis,* 10(4): 601-607.

Lee, J.A. (1988). Love styles. In R.J. Sternberg and M.L. Barnes (Eds.), *Psychology of love* (pp. 38-67). New Haven, CT: Yale University Press.

Maxwell, G.M. (1985). Behavior of lovers: Measuring closeness of relationships. *Journal of Social and Personal Relationships,* 2(2): 215-238.

Reddy, M.A. (Ed.) (1996). *Statistical abstract of the world* (Second edition). Detroit: Gale Research.

Sharlin, S.A. (1996). Long-term marriages in Israel. *Contemporary Family Therapy,* 18(2):225-242.

Sharlin, S.A. and Moin, V. (1997). *Long-term marriages: Comparative analysis between veterans and new immigrants in Israel.* Research Report. The Center For Research and Study of the Family, Haifa University.

Sternberg, R.J. (1986). A triangulating theory of love. *Psychological Review,* 93(2): 119-135.

Sternberg, R.J. (1988). Triangulating love. In R.J. Sternberg and M.L. Barnes (Eds.), *Psychology of love* (pp. 119-138). New Haven, CT: Yale University Press.

U.S. Bureau of the Census (1996). *Statistical abstracts of the United States* (116th edition). Washington, DC: Author.

Wynne, L.C. (1988). An epigenetic model of family processes. In C.J. Falicov (Ed.), *Family transitions: Continuity and change over the life cycle* (pp. 81-106). New York: Guilford Press.

Chapter 8

Bowen, M. (1988). *Family therapy in clinical practice.* New York: Jason Aronson.

Fennell, D.L. (1987). *Characteristics of long-term first marriages.* Paper presented at the 45th Annual American Association for Marriage and Family Therapy Conference, Chicago.

Gottman, J.M. (1994). *What predicts divorce? The relationship between marital processes and marital outcomes.* Hillsdale, NJ: Lawrence Erlbaum Associates.

Jacobson, M.P. and Margolin, G. (1979). A stimulus control model for change in behavioral marital therapy: Implication for contingency contracting. *Journal of Marriage and Family Counseling,* 4(1): 29-35.

Kaslow, F.W. (1981). Profile of the healthy family. *Interaction,* 4(1): 4-15.

Lauer, R., Lauer, J., and Kerr, S. (1990). The long-term marriage: Perceptions of stability and satisfaction. *International Journal of Aging and Human Development,* 31(3): 189-195.

Lewis, J., Beavers, W.R., Gossett, J.T., and Phillips, V.A. (1976). *No single thread: Psychological health in family systems.* New York: Brunner/Mazel.

Wallerstein, J.S. and Blakeslee, S. (1995). *The good marriage: How and why love lasts.* New York: Houghton Mifflin Co.

Walsh, F. (1982). *Normal family processes.* New York: Guilford.

Weishaus, S. and Field, D. (1988). A half century of marriage: Continuity or change? *Journal of Marriage and the Family,* 50(3): 763-774.

Index

Order Your Own Copy of
This Important Book for Your Personal Library!

TOGETHER THROUGH THICK AND THIN
A Multinational Picture of Long-Term Marriages

_____ in hardbound at $49.95 (ISBN: 0-7890-0492-5)

_____ in softbound at $19.95 (ISBN: 0-7890-0493-3)

COST OF BOOKS_____

OUTSIDE USA/CANADA/
MEXICO: ADD 20%_____

POSTAGE & HANDLING_____
(US: $4.00 for first book & $1.50
for each additional book
Outside US: $5.00 for first book
& $2.00 for each additional book)

SUBTOTAL_____

IN CANADA: ADD 7% GST_____

STATE TAX_____
(NY, OH & MN residents, please
add appropriate local sales tax)

FINAL TOTAL_____
(If paying in Canadian funds,
convert using the current
exchange rate. UNESCO
coupons welcome.)

☐ **BILL ME LATER:** ($5 service charge will be added)
(Bill-me option is good on US/Canada/Mexico orders only;
not good to jobbers, wholesalers, or subscription agencies.)

☐ Check here if billing address is different from
shipping address and attach purchase order and
billing address information.

Signature _____

☐ **PAYMENT ENCLOSED: $** _____

☐ **PLEASE CHARGE TO MY CREDIT CARD.**

☐ Visa   ☐ MasterCard   ☐ AmEx   ☐ Discover
☐ Diner's Club   ☐ Eurocard   ☐ JCB

Account # _____

Exp. Date _____

Signature _____

Prices in US dollars and subject to change without notice.

NAME _____

INSTITUTION _____

ADDRESS _____

CITY _____

STATE/ZIP _____

COUNTRY _____ COUNTY (NY residents only) _____

TEL _____ FAX _____

E-MAIL_____

May we use your e-mail address for confirmations and other types of information? ☐ Yes   ☐ No
We appreciate receiving your e-mail address and fax number. Haworth would like to e-mail or fax special
discount offers to you, as a preferred customer. **We will never share, rent, or exchange your e-mail
address or fax number.** We regard such actions as an invasion of your privacy.

Order From Your Local Bookstore or Directly From
The Haworth Press, Inc.

10 Alice Street, Binghamton, New York 13904-1580 • USA

TELEPHONE: 1-800-HAWORTH (1-800-429-6784) / Outside US/Canada: (607) 722-5857

FAX: 1-800-895-0582 / Outside US/Canada: (607) 772-6362

E-mail: getinfo@haworthpressinc.com

PLEASE PHOTOCOPY THIS FORM FOR YOUR PERSONAL USE.

www.HaworthPress.com

BOF00